THE DNA OF A MAN

MATT HALLOCK

Copyright © 2019 Matt Hallock

www.manwarriorking.com

www.matthallockauthor.com

All rights reserved. This book or any part thereof may not be reproduced or transmitted in any form, including information storage and retrieval systems, without permission in writing from the publisher, except for the use of brief quotations in a book review. For permission, visit www.matthallockauthor.com.

Unless otherwise indicated, all Scripture quotations are from The ESV® Bible (The Holy Bible, English Standard Version®), copyright © 2001 by Crossway. Used by permission. All rights reserved. Scripture quotations marked TPT are from The Passion Translation®. Copyright © 2017, 2018 by Passion & Fire Ministries, Inc. Used by permission. All rights reserved. ThePassionTranslation.com. Scripture quotations marked (NIV) are taken from the Holy Bible, New International Version®, NIV®. Copyright © 1973, 1978, 1984, 2011 by Biblica, Inc.™ Used by permission of Zondervan. All rights reserved worldwide. www.zondervan.com The "NIV" and "New International Version" are trademarks registered in the United States Patent and Trademark Office by Biblica, Inc.™ Scripture quotations marked NLT are taken from the Holy Bible, New Living Translation, copyright © 1996, 2004, 2015 by Tyndale House Foundation. Used by permission of Tyndale House Publishers, Inc., Carol Stream, Illinois 60188. All rights reserved. Scripture quotations marked NKJV are taken from the New King James Version®. Copyright © 1982 by Thomas Nelson. Used by permission. All rights reserved. Scripture quotations marked AMPC are taken from the Amplified® Bible (AMPC), Copyright © 1954, 1958, 1962, 1964, 1965, 1987 by The Lockman Foundation. Used by permission. www.Lockman.org

By the way, this book is not legal, medical, financial, psychological, horticultural, viticultural, marine biological, or any other professional advice. It is solely inspiration and motivation to my readers, conveying principles that I have seen to work well. The content is the opinion of the author. It is not eternal truth etched in stone (like the Ten Commandments). The author and publisher do not warranty or guarantee anything. Neither the author nor the publisher are liable for physical, psychological, emotional, financial, or commercial damages, including but not limited to special, incidental, consequential or other damages. You are responsible for your own choices, actions, and results. Welcome to the world of being an adult.

ISBN:

To my Father. You are beautiful and fierce. You are welcoming and dangerous. You are the author of my DNA.

To my dad. May the book I've written, the lives I change, and the man I am, bring honor to your name and tears of pride to your eyes.

To my grandpa, with Jesus. When you get a chance to read this, I'd love to hear your thoughts someday ... maybe as we're firing a few rounds at heaven's shooting range. I'm sure that's where you'll be.

To my wife. You married a man who still had a lot of boy in him. Thank you baby for challenging me to go higher, to reach further, to get stronger. Thank you for sharing yourself with me. Thank you for holding on to every dream in the face of every trial.

To my girls: Rebecca, Darcy, and Emerson. May I embody the message of this book so that you can flourish into warrior women of the Kingdom.

TABLE OF CONTENTS

Preface 1

Acknowledgements 5

This Is One Introduction You Don't Want

    to Skip 9

A Man of Identity

    The Search for Who You Are 23

    God's Opinion, Your Reality 37

    Welcome to...You 49

A Man of Principle

    Stop Pandering for Approval 65

    A Man of Your Word, Governed by

        Principle 75

    Master Your Allegiance 85

A Man on Mission

    Reclaiming Your Fire 103

    How to Be Legendary 119

Conclusion 135

PREFACE

Dear Man,

You are a man. You belong in our ranks. You are welcome here. We will not coddle you or help you find ways to try to make the immature boyishness in you feel better. We will instead hand you your sword and shield and empower you to silence the boy's whining by instead choosing manhood.

This book will open your eyes to the new type of existence as a man that you have not yet been taught. In fact, it's full of lessons that I wish I had known well before becoming a man (by age). If you ask me, I was not yet a man when I turned eighteen no matter what my tax return told me. I was on my way, sure. But in many important ways, I was still a boy.

I hope that this book is a catalyst to your own metamorphosis into true Godly manhood. May you become a confident, gritty, unshakeable, irresistible Man of the Kingdom as you embrace the DNA that Jesus re-injected into you when you said yes to him.

The message here has been born out of my growth, which was necessitated by, quite frankly, my doing marriage poorly. There came a point when I came face to face with my complete misunderstanding of what it means to be a husband. As I searched the "churchosphere" for help on becoming a man, I came up empty. Aside from key moments of intervention from a small number of Spirit-filled mentors, I kept finding advice that was not helping. The message conveyed by the larger church culture through blogs and books and podcasts simply didn't apply to me. I was already doing everything they were saying, but things were still choppy. I was still hurting—floundering, even. And this advice certainly wasn't creating the spark between my wife and me that I was looking for.

Preface

It was as if my operating system was wrong. The "software" that I had been blessed to receive from ministries and ministering mentors was good. It provided pieces of the puzzle, and it could have had more results. In fact, it has had great results for many. But for me—and now I know for many other men—that software simply couldn't move the needle until I went deeper and performed a complete overhaul of my masculinity paradigm.

So, I turned to the "manosphere," the term that has been coined to refer to the collection of work emerging in the secular world about reclaiming true masculinity—though without Jesus in the process. Surprisingly, the manosphere helped me way more than the churchosphere. The "secular" books and blogs that I found finally taught me things like manly confidence; a healthy, non-codependent emotional independence from my wife; and the value of having a mission as a man. God used these sources to give me that operating system change that I needed, and I started to see new and lasting change.

During this manosphere learning period, God also blessed me with a fantastic counselor, a mighty man of God who showed me that it **is** indeed possible to follow Jesus, to walk as he walked, while at the same time growing in the true qualities of a man. (The two are not mutually exclusive, though I had begun to wonder.) Furthermore, he connected me with my DNA as a man and gave me marriage guidance that began a fresh process of Holy Spirit transformation.

But finding this type of more-than-standard wisdom that I was receiving from him was incredibly difficult, so I saw the huge gaping hole that someone needed to fill: men need help becoming men, true men, not nice guys who try to constantly appease their wives, hoping beyond hope that somehow she notices all of their effort. But also, men need that help from a Kingdom man, from someone who is running hard after Jesus. From a man who believes in the supernatural and sees God do miracles in everyday life. From a man who understands that we need, on the one hand, to take ownership of our lives, and, on the other hand, to depend one hundred percent on Jesus for absolutely everything.

So was born this book and the Man Warrior King ministry. Be excited because this is the first book in a series of three. The next two are *The DNA of a Warrior* and *The DNA of a King*. They, too, will push you toward the man God designed you to be.

Think of this book as your opportunity to wake up out of the dual Matrix. First, wake up from the commonly taught weak, nice, passive, and self-pitiful form of "manhood" that has been keeping you stuck and disrupting your marriage. Step into, instead, a God-ordained manhood that ripples with strength, confidence, initiative, and action.

Second, wake up from a lifeless and bland faith that has replaced the presence of God with beliefs about God. Instead, experience an alive and powerful daily encounter with him. This is the crux of our existence. Everything else that you feel has gone wrong in your life is second fiddle to your connection with him. And focusing your effort on fixing those areas of pain will only leave you frustrated until you are healthy in who you are as a man and who you are as a son of the Father. You can either fight your battles on your own, or you can reorient your whole operating system so that you position yourself to receive the aid in battle of Jesus himself.

I opt for the second. How about you?

Much love, Brother,

Matt Hallock

P.S. If you want to talk more about all this, need someone to pray with you, or would like a square kick in the butt to propel you forward, then see the back of the book for how to get in touch with me. You're not alone.

ACKNOWLEDGEMENTS

God, I acknowledge you in the creation of this book, yes, but more importantly, in the process that you and I have walked together as I've grown out of boyishness and into manhood. I'm sorry for doubting that you're with me. How foolish. You caught me in the beginning and never let me go from that day forward. You have fathered me. You have "pottered" me, this little piece of clay. I am the work of your hand, and I carry your image proudly through all of my endless days.

Dad, the other one whose image I carry. Thank you for teaching me laughter and joy. Thank you for investing in my baseball games and showing me I'm a better infielder than outfielder. Thank you for playing wiffle ball with me, jumping on the trampoline with me, wrestling in the living room with me, and bringing appliance boxes home for me. Thank you for letting me roam through your animal hospital like royalty. And thank you for teaching me that real men give up their sports cars when their son is in crisis. I love you.

Dennis, you were the Coast Guard swimmer who came just as I was about to go under. You have taught me real, true, gritty, messy, glorious manliness. You, Dennis, are the guy in the room whose posse I would want to join. You are "that guy," the one who would have made me think, "I wish I was manly like that guy." I don't think that anymore, because you've helped me become "that guy." I am honored to be counseled by you. To be corrected by you. To be fathered by you. Thank you for teaching me every lesson I wrote in this book. I owe you.

Frank, thank you for being my second dad. Thank you for letting me spend a freakishly large amount of time at your house with your family. Thank you for treating me as your fourth son and for giving me a home of men and boys

Acknowledgements

when I needed it most. Thank you for modeling for me a man who loves the Lord and loves his family, both with every block of his DNA. I have grown up under your care. I have fished with you. I have hiked and camped and roasted stuff over the fire with you. And I have suffered with you. I hope my mansion is next to yours.

Josh, Elijah, and David, thanks for being my brothers. Thanks for making me tough and not a weak little cry-baby. Thanks for adventuring with me and encouraging me to break more rules than I would have on my own. Thanks for the countless yards we ran through, the cars we threw water balloons at, the people we spied on, and the mountains we climbed. Josh, I'm sorry we left you to take the fall. I'm here to return the favor if, one day, you need me to do so. Thank you Josh for being my brother and advocate and supporter in these recent years. And you're right, "Brothers don't shake hands…"

Mr. Bowman, at perhaps the most pivotal time of my growing up, you were there for me. You "manned" life and let me observe and learn from you. You invited me into your circle, when I felt like an outsider. You took me under your wing and believed in me when I wondered if I even belonged. And you forgave me and restored me when I lied to you. You taught me what passion looks like in the Kingdom. You taught me what it means to "be married to Jesus." You are priceless to me.

Mr. Tarr and Mr. Skaff, thank you for sending me into adulthood with the affirmation and acceptance of true men of God under my belt. Thank you for loving me day in and day out as I was finding my footing as a man. You didn't have to love me, but you did. This is one life of hundreds that you changed for the good. I believe that God could honor each of you for a thousand years just because of the impact you've had on me, one little person. Imagine how much he will honor you when he shows us all how you've touched so many lives.

Kevin T., you are my brother. You have seen me at my most real in the highest and the lowest, and you of all other men and friends have walked pretty much every step with me. Your brotherhood is a gift to me. You are a real man.

Kevin J., you too are my brother. Sorry I invited you to live in a sketchy house in college, and sorry we got invaded. I know it wasn't totally my fault, but sorry anyway. You and your bride have supported us so well. You have loved us so well. You have accepted us for who we are. Thank you.

Mike, I wish we were still down the hall from each other. I wish we were still dishing out the Spirit together, day in and day out. I have always respected you and wanted to be like you since we met. You carry a confident joy, a steady manly strength, that not many others have. I want to find our next mission to tackle together. We make a dang good team.

THIS IS ONE INTRODUCTION YOU DON'T WANT TO SKIP

> Now it happened in the month of Chislev, in the twentieth year, as I was in Susa the citadel, that Hanani, one of my brothers, came with certain men from Judah. And I asked them concerning the Jews who escaped, who had survived the exile, and concerning Jerusalem. And they said to me, "The remnant there in the province who had survived the exile is in great trouble and shame. The wall of Jerusalem is broken down, and its gates are destroyed by fire."
> As soon as I heard these words I sat down and wept and mourned for days, and I continued fasting and praying before the God of heaven.
> **Nehemiah 1: 1-4**

Don't worry. The book you are about to read is brimming with joy, hope, and strength. It will leave you with a new set of lenses through which you'll be able to see your life. It will give you reasons why you've been hurting. It will show you God's path out of pain and into life as he meant it: full, joyful, light. The book itself will not transform you, but as I write these words I'm asking the Holy Spirit to infuse them with himself, so that he can bring transformation through them.

So you're in for something good. And if you jump all in, willing to let go of how you've been going at life up until now, you will find strength, confidence, drive, and passion like you've never known. Or maybe you have known it, but it's gone missing for a while. And you haven't been able to figure out how to find it all again. And your life is hurting because of it.

Christian men. Men in the church. Men who follow Jesus and truly want to know him. The message in this book is to all of you—to all of us. That said, the situation we're starting in—you and me, together—is pretty rough. Let's be real with each other. Much like the state of Jerusalem in the first few words from the book of Nehemiah, above, the state of our own city doesn't look good. Like Jerusalem, the state of men in the church is "in great trouble and shame." We are "broken down" and our "gates are destroyed by fire."

And even as you read these words you know this is true. They match with that gaping hole that you feel and haven't been able to close. There's something wrong, you feel, with the life that you've been experiencing. It seems somehow smaller, more limited, more bogged down than you would have expected. You read the New Testament and you find adventure, risk, valor, heroism. You see men and women living supernaturally in another realm, God's kingdom, doing things like healing the sick, preaching to angry mobs, surviving snake bites and beatings and shipwrecks, talking to angels, and going into the whole world to make disciples.

Why then, you wonder, are you stuck simply trying to survive? Jesus didn't assure us that he came to help us squeak by. He didn't promise barely enough power and presence. He promised more than enough. He promised overflow of power and life. Remember how he said that rivers of living water would flow out of us (John 7:38)?

Well, where are they?

And how are you supposed to concern yourself with going out and changing the world for his kingdom and his glory when you can't make ends meet from month to month, your kids are going off the deep end, you are painfully disconnected from your wife, and you wake up each morning with poisonous fog that dampens your thinking and your emotions?

Or perhaps you are managing to go out and "reach the world for Jesus," but you're not winning the inner battle. The outer "success" masks the inner struggle against despair and unfulfillment. You are going through all the right motions and you're somehow lacking the vibrant life-giving connection with Jesus that you see in men like Moses, Abraham, Joshua, and Paul. Maybe in this case, things in your life are enviable to most outsiders, but the one closest to you, your wife, still feels the sting of your faltering inner man and the impotence of your weakened, weary, and wounded spirit.

Here's what you and I are going to do: we are going to climb out of this state of "trouble and shame" and we are going to rebuild our broken down city. We are going to pick up brick after crumbled brick and rebuild the wall that used to protect us (Proverbs 25:28, Isaiah 58:12), that used to give us our strength. We are going to reclaim the heritage that once was, and still is, ours to lay hold of. We are going to regain the power, authority, and ability to go forward and conquer in the name of Jesus. We are going to learn to stand in confidence and conviction once again. Essentially, we are going to become who we've always been: strong and valiant sons of God the King.

What's happened, though, is that we have forgotten all of this. We have abandoned both who we are and who we follow, just like the people of Judah did. And so, like them, we've been thrown into exile not by one powerful foreign nation, but by many smaller but equally powerful idols. For some of us, the idol is our success. For some it is our physique. For others it is our wife. And for all of us, it is our self.

How did we arrive here? How, when we are supposed to model God's character and Jesus's power on the earth, did we end up wounded, weak, and somehow missing the boat of God's victorious-sounding promises?

FATHERS

We have not been fathered well. I think back over the course of my life, especially those formative teenage years—and even into college—and I can think of very few young men who were truly secure, truly confident. The ones I can think of were not cocky, arrogant, or mean bullies. They were simply sincere. Sincere in confidence and in self-assuredness.

These few "elite" young men among us had fathers who were present and authentically invested in their lives. They actively and consistently demonstrated their care and love for their sons. Conversely, many of the other kids my age would talk like they didn't have good relationships with their dads at all. It was as if they carried an underlying disdain for their dads, rooted in hurt and bitterness.

So yes, our limping culture of manhood does suffer immensely from this lack of active and powerful fathering. You and I unfortunately reap the consequences of the generations that came before us—consequences that include this pervasive ignorance concerning the vital lessons of manhood.

This Is One Introduction You Don't Want to Skip

For me, there was a very significant part of my life, where heartbreakingly, for both of us, my dad wasn't able to be present. During those years of middle and high school, without him there to affirm, secure, and guide me, I went through a significant period of discouragement and depression. I was confused and alone and left wondering, How do I actually live as a man? How do I do life? There's no one around whom I trust to show me.

I'm deeply thankful that the God of angel armies stepped into that intimate place of my life and began to father me. He showed me, and is still showing me, what it means to live in my full masculinity both in this world and in his Kingdom. He showed me how to follow him as a son who lives from that previously elusive spirit of acceptance and security.

Unfortunately, there have been times along my journey when I stepped out of that intimate Father-son connection, and those times delayed my growth, literally stunting my development into true manhood. In fact, in some ways, I stayed a boy for years—particularly in relating to my wife, in husbanding her as a strong and confident man should. I can certainly concur with the nearly-cliche concept that marriage is like a mirror that reflects (and magnifies) your character. My marriage was the primary arena of my life where my places of immaturity played out.

I'm convinced that if my dad had been able to play a more consistent role in my upbringing and the shaping of my character, then I probably would have made some very different choices that would have instead accelerated my growth into a man of strength, honor, and power in the kingdom.

I know my story is not unique. You and I are in this together. You too, have likely needed something from your own dad, or the other men in your life, that you simply did not receive. This is not an indictment against those men who have gone before us. This is not a "Poor me, blame my dad" moment. This is an acknowledgement of the simple fact that there is more for you and me. There is more, but only one Father is able to give it to us. So we will run after him, and him alone.

VILLAINS

The cultural villainization of manhood that has come about in the last fifty or sixty years is another reason for the pain we experience as we fight to become real men. The term "toxic masculinity" gets thrown around, spreading the notion that certain aspects of normal healthy masculinity are actually detrimental to our world and to the poor unfortunate souls who have to put up with real men. This is sad, dangerous, and it grieves the heart of God. He made both men and women to live as fully themselves, in all of their unique and sometimes uncomfortable glory.

But we've grown up in this overly feminized culture where we've been taught that certain facets—good facets—of our masculinity need to be covered over. They need to be guarded against. We men are often seen as the actual enemies in the world. And true! For much of history, men have oppressed, pillaged, stiff-armed, and degraded women. That is absolutely true. But I would contend that those scars on history are from men living as immature boys—men living in destructive arrogance, self-protection, and downright sin. Those are not examples of "men being men," but they are examples of "boys being boys."

Today, a character trait like aggression is typically seen as negative. But without this aggression, America would not be a country (sorry to my British friends). And let's not forget the heroes of the Bible whom we remember as heroes primarily because of their aggression: the mighty men of David, Joshua, Caleb, Nehemiah, and many of the judges and kings and prophets. Aggression is what defends a home when intruders break in. Aggression is what sees injustice and does something to stop it.

SINNERS

Even more tragic than this cultural degradation of manhood though, is what the church has done. We have accepted a Gospel message that causes us to look down on ourselves. It may not be as blatant as, "Hey, man. Think of yourself as garbage!" But there is this bent in our cultural Christianity that tells us very sneakily that we are worthless. We leave church thinking that, thankfully, God would be so kind as to condescend and come and save us, because, boy oh boy!, we sure are pieces of garbage! Just "sinners saved by grace."

When we begin to look down on ourselves this way and to equate ourselves with actual scum, then our masculinity gets lumped into this low esteem. We begin to question things that are good in us. If we are such disgusting sinners, even after Jesus supposedly saves us and washes us clean, injecting us with his righteousness, then everything about us must be abhorrent.

Not that everything in us is good. Sure, there are places where you're messed up and need mending. There are places where I need to grow and change. But in all this introspection and self-examination, looking for all the ways we need to grow and become more like Jesus, we've massively missed it. The gospel actually enables us to rise up into everything we were meant to be, into the fullness of ourselves. It doesn't leave us broken. It calls us worthy, whole, righteous, good, powerful, valuable. All the things that feel un-Christian and arrogant when we venture to say them about ourselves.

That's right, I challenge you: begin asking the Lord to change how you think about you. You are absolutely worthy, righteous, good, and powerful. Not on your own. Not floating off into self-centeredness, but fully dependent on Jesus for everything you are and have. And since you have been restored into your original created identity by Jesus, you are pretty darn impressive. The world is blessed by your presence.

WHAT YOU AND I ARE GOING TO DO ABOUT IT

Here's what we are going to do about the situation we are in. Here's how we are going to stand up and take back the victorious masculine living that God intended for us to live in. We aren't going to solve the grand socio-cultural problems of fatherless generations, over-feminization, and churchwide self-degradation. Nor are we going to work on fixing any of the external things that are going wrong in your life. I'm not going to give you "Kingdom strategies" for business, parenting, marriage, or ministry. Not that those things are bad, but I believe they are premature. They are pieces of a house that can only be used **after** there's a solid foundation. They are the inner buildings of the broken down city that can only be restored **after** we've rebuilt the wall that will secure it all.

Instead, we are going to the core of your being, to your DNA. DNA is the famed (thanks to high school biology class) double helix that carries within its microscopic structure all of the information needed to build you into the man that you are. The unequaled power that resides in this small miraculous blueprint is staggering. If you want to truly change a man's physical nature, this would be where to do that. You can change his hair color temporarily by dyeing it black. Or, if this is even possible, you can dive into his DNA, alter some building blocks, and forever permanently make him a black-haired man.

The kingdom of heaven operates in a man's life and brings total transformation only as it works from the inside out.

> "The kingdom of heaven is like a grain of mustard seed that a man took and sowed in his field. It is the smallest of all seeds, but when it has grown it is larger than all the garden plants and becomes a tree, so that the birds of the air come and make nests in its branches." (**Matthew 13:31-32**)

This is why we are not looking to fix all of the possible pain points that have reared up in your life. We're not looking to temporarily dye your hair. We are looking for permanent and truly powerful transformation that does not wear out and cannot be undone. Your DNA must be transformed to match the DNA of the Father before any lasting transformation of worth can take place in those painful external circumstances.

Thankfully, Jesus has done the work of DNA transformation already. But, like those inhabitants of the city of Jerusalem in Judah, we have forgotten who we truly are. We have forgotten our heavenly genetics, the heritage passed down to us by our Father, and we have adopted the old, lesser, poisonous ways of unredeemed manhood. Consequently we have become weak, cowardly, emotionally dependent on our wives, and easily swayed by the storms of life.

MARRIAGE GETS SPECIAL TREATMENT

The one exception, if you can call it that, to my rule of not fixing the external pieces of your life, is marriage. While we are definitely not going to be working on "fixing" your marriage, the kind of entire-life-wholeness and healing that we will be working toward as we rediscover our manly God-given DNA will undoubtedly change how you do marriage. It will change the way you conduct yourself as husband and the way you relate with your wife.

Throughout this book, you will read about the principles of your transformation into a real man—a man of the kingdom—in relation to who you are as a husband. We will discuss openly how your wounded and broken way of living has damaged your marriage and hurt your wife. And we will openly discuss the opportunities for healing your marriage that are available to you when you live as Jesus is calling you to live.

Why the focus on marriage? Why not talk about the other areas of life that some men struggle in—money, work, ministry, etc.? What about those guys who need help with those other things?

Several reasons for you:

First, marriage is a frustratingly fantastic magnifying glass of a man's inner world. Even when the rest of life looks good on the outside, it's difficult for a man's marriage to be good when his inner world is locked in unhealth and he's not connected to his true DNA.

Second, if we were to look at our lives as a diagram of concentric circles, I believe that marriage would be the second circle out from the center of a man's connection to himself and Jesus. Of all external features in this life, marriage is closest to our core.

Third, for too many men, their marriages are the primary source of pain and therefore bitterness and therefore smallness of living. They are derailed and distracted from their mission on the earth, to know Jesus and make him known, by the struggles they have with their wives. That being the case, our view and approach to marriage needs a massive overhaul. It warrants the extra attention.

Fourth, marriage is powerful in the kingdom and therefore dangerous to the darkness. Let's get this thing right, men, so that we can get back to kicking butt and taking names, together side by side with our wives.

Fifth, marriage has been a major, if not *the* major impetus and canvas of my own transformation from immature boyhood into manhood.

DISCOVERING OUR DNA

So, what exactly is the DNA of a man? The blueprint, though simple and concise, is powerful. It carries with it a supernatural grace that will supercharge your living. God himself will flow through it and heal your places of emotional and physical pain. He will, with this blueprint, break chains of emotional paralysis that you've been powerless to break on your own. He will alleviate and heal the pain that you've endured in those vulnerable places of your life. And he will give you a new power in life to live on the offense, to advance and take ground for his kingdom.

Sounds good, doesn't it?

It's time for us to do something—to take intentional, incisive, restorative action. When Nehemiah heard about the sorry state of his homeland, he was so deeply cut that he abandoned everything and then risked everything to go back to the land of his fathers and rebuild.

> Then I said to them, "You see the trouble we are in, how Jerusalem lies in ruins with its gates burned. Come, let us build the wall of Jerusalem, that we may no longer suffer derision."
> And I told them of the hand of my God that had been upon me for good, and also of the words that the king had spoken to me. And they said, ***"Let us rise up and build."*** So they strengthened their hands for the good work. (Nehemiah 2:17-18)

Rise up and build. It's time to discover your DNA.

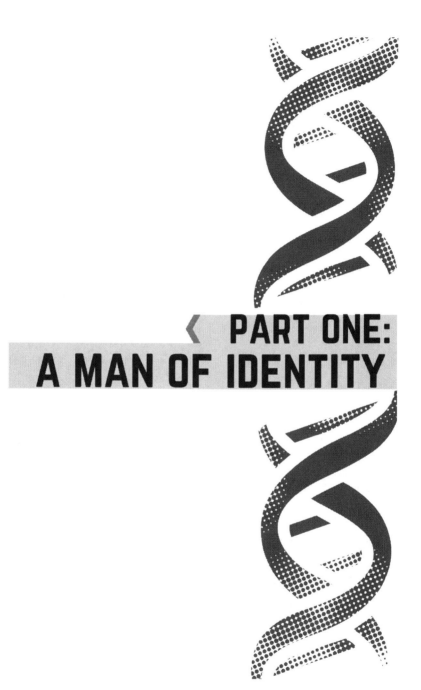

PART ONE:
A MAN OF IDENTITY

"Being a male is a matter of birth. Being a man is a matter of choice."

-Edwin Louis Cole[2]

1

THE SEARCH FOR WHO YOU ARE

IMAGINE WATCHING A father and his boy walking down the street together. Notice how they have the same gait, the same general body shape, the same sway to their shoulders. Notice how that same little boy's facial features look like a thirty-years-ago version of his dad. The boy stands in the bathroom each morning combing his hair like his dad. He "shaves" like his dad. He laughs at all the same jokes that his dad laughs at (even when he has no idea what they mean), and his laugh sounds like his dad's laugh. In fact, the boy even smells like his dad.

Strangers passing by can tell that this little boy belongs to this man. The two, while obviously different, are also simultaneously one and the same. Cut from the same cloth.

For myself, I don't see my dad very much. He lives a couple states over and up from me, doing his thing with the great wild beasts of the north. But when we talk on the phone, the resemblance of my dad that I carry is striking even to me. The way I say certain phrases, the tone I use at certain points in conversation, the way I laugh—they are all spot-on representations of my dad.

When he and I talk, it reminds me of conversations I have with various clients where, as I'm going over material with them, I ask them "Okay?" to see if they've been following along with me.

This in turn takes me back to my days as a young boy when I was lucky enough to be able to join my dad at work at his veterinarian hospital. In addition to making friends with the dogs and cats that would file through his expert care, I'd also sit in on his client meetings and listen as he would calm and comfort the otherwise troubled and worried pet owners. He would always use the exact same "okay" with the exact same intonation.

No matter how far the distance between us and how long it has been since those days of early childhood, my dad is my dad. He is my heritage. Who I am today as a man stems from this man's character and DNA, and I was residing in his being long before I was even born. I am like him, and I, in honor, carry his image.

This may or may not be how you **feel** about yourself and God, but it is absolutely one hundred percent truth. You are like your Father. The spirit world watches you and notices that you look frighteningly similar to the one who made you. You, in all of your masculinity, were created—literally crafted—as a masterpiece, carrying the very image and likeness of God Almighty, the Dread Champion (Jeremiah 20:11), the one before whom waters tremble and mountains crumble.

What would it feel like to know—I mean actually **know**—this is your Father? This is your bloodline. This is your heritage. If, in the same way that a boy carries the aura of his dad, you carry the presence of your Father, then is it such a huge stretch to believe that waters should tremble and mountains should crumble before you as well? Not because you too are God, but because the earth sees God inside of you. It sees his seal of approval on you and understands that you, contradictory to all of our logic and overly religious conceptions, carry his power and authority.

IDENTITY IN THE BEGINNING

The first building block of your masculine DNA is *Identity*. Merriam Webster defines *Identity* as,

***

condition or character as to who a person or what a thing is; the qualities, beliefs, etc., that distinguish or identify a person or thing[1]

In other words, your Identity is your essence, the mixture of qualities, both tangible and intangible, that are inseparable from you and make up who you are. Your Identity is your core: your man-ness, your you-ness. But, as we've seen, your Identity does not simply exist within you completely unconnected to anyone or anything else. It is not independent, nor is it self-generating. Your Identity as a man has been bestowed on you, and you did nothing to either qualify for or disqualify yourself from its blessings. It simply is, irrespective of your behavior from one moment to the next.

A fascinating additional definition for *Identity* that Merriam Webster gives is this:

exact likeness in nature or qualities [1]

So we have in a single word the tension between your uniqueness, the core of who you are, and also your likeness as a son of your Father. To be a Man of Identity in God's kingdom is to be a man who knows both who he has been uniquely created to be and the one whom he has been finely crafted to resemble. Whose image he is to bear. Whose likeness he cannot help but exude from his being. When you connect with your heavenly heritage and begin to understand the overwhelming nature of being a son of the Father, it will give exponentially more value to your own nature. Your sonship is what gives your uniqueness incredible worth. You were made to be a man who knows his worth and his place in the world. A man who knows where he comes from and whose image he carries.

Look with me at Genesis chapter 1, verse 26 and 27:

> Then God said, "Let us make man in our image, after our likeness. And let them have dominion over the fish of the sea and over the birds of the heavens and over the livestock and over all the earth and over every creeping thing that creeps on the earth." So God created man in his own image, in the image of God he created him; male and female

he created them.

It is with laser-like purpose that this affirmation from God of Adam's Identity as his image-bearer comes before the specific recounting of Adam's creation out of the dust. You, friend, were intentionally identified as God's son even before your physical formation.

> "Before I formed you in the womb I knew you, and before you were born I consecrated you; I appointed you a prophet to the nations." (Jeremiah 1:5)

Do you see? Your Identity was established before you even came around to screw it up. There's nothing that you can do to shake this! You can live outside of it. You can live disconnected from Jesus and the Father and therefore not experience the ramifications of this Identity. But you can never change who you were meant to be. And you certainly cannot cause God to regret how he created you.

WHEN IDENTITY IS LOST

When we don't know who we are, we carry in our bones an insatiable hunger to be defined, to know our purpose, to know exactly our place of belonging. That's why these questions persistently haunt us: *Where do I fit in? DO I fit in? Am I even acceptable? Am I lovable? Am I worthy of someone's attention, affection, adoration, admiration? Am I worthy to be honored?*

BASEBALL: MY SEARCH FOR IDENTITY

This search for our Identity can pull us in any number of directions. For instance, when I was younger, I loved baseball. Absolutely loved it. I knew for sure that my passion for the game would take me to the big leagues. In fact, my dream was to be a professional baseball player/traveling evangelist. I wanted to be the next Billy Sunday (though at the time I had never heard of the famous professional ballplayer/traveling evangelist). I thought, "Hey, if I could be an all-star-soon-to-be-Hall-of-Famer, then who wouldn't listen to me when I preached? Right?" My fame and amazing baseball skills would make people respect me and value my opinion.

The DNA of a Man

I played baseball for ten years, from the age of eight to the age of seventeen. I wasn't aware of this during my "career," but now that I look back, I can see that I found way too much of my self-worth through baseball. I cared so much about how well I played that I psyched myself out of actually wanting to go to the games. What if I didn't get a hit? What if I struck out? What if I made an error in the field? The weight was too much to deal with.

So I would hope for rain delays or for some other reason the game would have to be cancelled—maybe I'd get sick, or injured, or I'd have to take my cat to the vet—anything to alleviate my anxiety. Obviously, the games usually happened unobstructed by my wishful thinking. If I had a good game—a couple hits, a few RBI, a defensive highlight, etc.—then I could relax and feel proud of myself. I could accept myself. But if I didn't have a good game—maybe I went hitless, struck out once or twice, etc.—I cannot describe to you how depressed I would become. During the games, I'd throw my helmet. I'd cry on the bench. I'd cry on the field. After the games I'd pout, cry, and be quite honestly a punk to anyone around.

The sad thing is, I wasn't alone. There were many other kids who also went through this hell. Too many. Too many lost and hurting young boys out there trying to find their meaning from a game.

Going into high school, I'd put in hours of practice on my own behind my house on the little grass field where I set up a net and a tee. I'd throw dozens of balls into the net, working on my pretty weak arm strength. And I'd hit ball after ball off the tee into the net, honing my swing, analyzing it for weaknesses and looking to constantly improve my hitting power.

It all sounds good, like I was a diligent kid working hard at his passion, but it never paid off like I wanted. I never did perform as well as I knew I could, or should. And I was not happy. Even though I wanted to play baseball, I hated it at the same time.

Does this sound familiar to you? You want to perform well at work, for instance. But even though you're trying with every bit of grit and determination you know how to muster, you're not happy. You want to be married to your wife, but you're not truly feeling fulfilled and at peace in your relationship. You want to be a dad—a good dad—to your kids, but you're not feeling like you can be, and it's actually a source of anxiety rather than joy. In all of these, you are not living up to the standard that you envisioned.

Throughout my baseball career, I'd observe other players—friends of mine. They too worked hard at their game. They too might put in hours of their own practice, like me. But they played better. A lot better. And the frustrating thing was, they didn't seem to care as much as I did. I cared more, but they played better and had more fun.

How is that fair?

It's not. It is not fair.

But it is consistent. It's consistent with the laws of the kingdom that Jesus himself set up.

> "For whoever would save his life will lose it, but whoever loses his life for my sake will save it." (Luke 9:24)

See, fairness doesn't matter at all. What matters is that my friends had a healthier view of themselves and of the game. They weren't trying to find their Identity, to "save their lives," in the game of baseball. I, however, was. And in doing so, I was going against the ways of Jesus. That's the single reason why their hard work paid off and mine didn't.

What's interesting is that many of those kids had dads that affirmed them and gave them a place of belonging. Their dads helped define these kids' Identities (outside of the game of baseball) so that they had no driving urge to find themselves through the game. Meanwhile, I was looking for my own Identity, my own value and belonging within baseball. I was looking to baseball to provide me with my meaning, and I consequently crippled my performance, sabotaged my joy, and lost my confidence.

FIND YOURSELF, HEAL YOUR MARRIAGE

Just as I did with baseball, when a man puts excessive pressure on things that are otherwise good, those things actually become a source of emotional and spiritual death. Gold is good. But when God's people turned that gold into a god that they then worshipped, it became death and separation from

God. When I worshipped my baseball performance, baseball became a joy-stealing burden.

Obviously, the lack of Identity in and of itself, aside from any other human involvement, wounds our core, but when we forever join ourselves to a woman without having settled these questions beforehand, that same wound becomes massive. And it oozes onto her. I'm guessing, judging by all of your best and most fervent efforts to "win your wife's heart," this oozing wound is definitely not the kind of legacy you want to leave as a husband.

Are you worshipping your wife and looking for the wrong things from her? She is an easy target for your desperate need for worth and validation. And if your arrows hit their mark, then your marriage is in for a bumpy ride.

This marital death trap is especially a risk if, as young men, our fathers didn't initiate us into being Men of Identity. In the absence of that masculine fatherly affirmation, we naturally tend to look for our identities from women—first our mothers, and then later our wives. We learn that if we cannot be loved and accepted and secured in the world of men, our mothers are often eagerly waiting to assume that role and fill the gap that was left. She is the other parent, after all. So she's the natural choice.

But as we grow up and move out of the house, if we haven't learned this dynamic and been healed of its damage—if we haven't grown out of the immaturity that the whole thing is wrapped in—then we often transfer this search for validation over to our wives. This is exactly why God's declaration of Adam's Identity came not just before Adam existed, but also before he encountered Eve for the first time. It's vital to your ability to thrive that you have this understanding of your Identity outside of any other person, especially the most important person in your life: your wife. For a very blessed few of us, we thankfully learn to become a Man of Identity **before** ever meeting our wives. But unfortunately, because this primal masculine awareness has been long covered over, many or most of us do not learn who we really are before getting married. So we look for our Identity from the new most important woman in our existence, and we assign her the life-sucking job of providing our definition, value, and belonging. We mistakenly look to her to transform us into a Man of Identity.

Once we fall into this toxic pattern, everything that we try to do to help our marriage—the stuff we do to evoke romance and to create connection and intimacy—will not work. Our demonstrations of "love" (which is actually need) will go nowhere and will actually create more resentment rather than restore intimacy.

It's like trying to clean your house when you yourself are caked in wet dripping mud that you're just slinging all over the floors, walls, and furniture. You can be using all the right cleaning tools and sprays and brooms and mops and whatever. You can be going through all the right behaviors, and even doing it with joy and gusto. But you yourself are going to be getting the house dirty—constantly. You need to clean up your own self first. And this issue of getting rooted in your Identity outside of your wife, and apart from all other sources who are not Jesus, is the place where you need to begin. This is why so much of marital healing doesn't involve the marriage at all. It involves you.

MARKS OF A MAN WITH NO IDENTITY

So, what does this actually look like, for a man to live without his proper Identity? First, he lives, or we live, afraid. We look at the world as a threatening place, a place of cold hard reality that only a select few are able to navigate safely. In marriage, this fear causes us to see our wife as a threat rather than a blessing. We fear making her upset and shifting her delicate mood into the "dark place." We fear her disapproval of us if we were to ever do anything so audacious as being ourselves.

Second, without Identity we live dependent. We depend on external circumstances for our well-being and our sense of security and worth. For husbands, this manifests in our unhealthy emotional suckling at our wife's breast. Graphic and uncomfortable and maybe inappropriate, I know. But that's what we're doing. We feel as though we cannot survive without her, without that life-giving connection to her. We need her in order to feel okay. And yet we somehow don't understand why she doesn't seem attracted to us and the manly valor that we could have sworn was in us somewhere.

Third, without Identity we live depressed. We do not have a deep abiding sense that we are worth something—anything—and so we of course cannot be happy. We cannot worship God with abandon. We cannot carry ourselves in confident lightheartnedness. We bring a downcast atmosphere into our home and our family.

Fourth, without Identity we live small and quiet because Identity is the fundamental need of every human. Before all else we must know who we are and where we belong. If we don't have this, then we cannot waste our time changing the world. We're too busy trying to get ourselves to the point where we can even begin to think about things outside of ourselves. How do you think this makes our wives feel, when we husbands are consumed constantly with ourselves. We are making our major goal each day to merely patch up the holes in our own ship rather than to patch up the holes in hers. We cannot properly love and secure her from a place of our own insecure selfishness. This is not conducive to the marriage you and I want, one of warmth, vulnerability, and passion.

THE CULPRIT

If this is you, you're likely throwing your hands up, banging your head on the table and asking God and anyone else who can hear you, "How did this happen? How did I get here? How did Identity, or lack thereof, cause me to poison my marriage when all I've wanted to do is help it flourish?"

Great questions. I'm glad you asked.

Because it's time for you to stop being a lost and scared little boy disconnected from your place in the Father, trying helplessly to find love and peace and passion in your home. You wonder why your wife seems cold and resentful. You wonder what happened to the dating dynamic of ancient ages past. The answer is that your wife is looking for a real man, a man who knows who he is. A Man of Identity who, from that knowledge, draws strength and solid confidence. A man who can lead and provide and cover and **give** life rather than suck it out of her.

Without a solid Identity and awareness that you are an astounding image-bearer of your Creator, you've begun to search for some other, lesser, image to carry. You perhaps unknowingly, but still just as sinfully, have abandoned God as the one who defines you, the bestower of your meaning and purpose. He is no longer your very source of life.

Did you catch that? Did **I** catch that? You and I need to wake up and man up and realize that this loss of Identity is not just some wicked plot that we have fallen victim to. We are not allowed anymore to sit in the corner and baby our wounds, trying desperately to get the pain to go away. We are men. Pain is part of our existence. We choose to let it own us, or we choose to let it feed us. You make the call.

Think back to the introduction a few pages ago and consider Nehemiah's response to the news that Jerusalem was in shambles. He didn't sit there and say, "But God! It's not my fault. They did this to us. I had nothing to do with it. Rescue me!" Nope. Instead he acts like a man and takes some responsibility for the heartbreaking situation that was not even his fault. He identifies himself with his people, and he owns the sin.

> "Let your ear be attentive and your eyes open, to hear the prayer of your servant that I now pray before you day and night for the people of Israel your servants, confessing the sins of the people of Israel, which we have sinned against you. Even I and my father's house have sinned. We have acted very corruptly against you and have not kept the commandments, the statutes, and the rules that you commanded your servant Moses." (Nehemiah 1:6-7)

We have sinned, you and I. We have done this! We are not victims here, we are perpetrators. Therefore, the first step for us to take is not to find the culprit, but to repent for being that very culprit. God warns us,

"But my people have changed their glory
    for that which does not profit.
Be appalled, O heavens, at this;
    be shocked, be utterly desolate,
declares the Lord,
for my people have committed two evils:
they have forsaken me,
    the fountain of living waters,
and hewed out cisterns for themselves,

broken cisterns that can hold no water." (Jeremiah 2:11-13)

All of our frantic searching for Identity from things in life other than Jesus has led to us literally giving back the gift of glory that God had previously instilled in us.

We essentially say, "Nope. No thank you, Jesus. I do not need, nor do I want to share in your glory and have you call that glory my own. I do not want to drink from your unstoppable supply of life-giving water that would not only sustain me but also heal me and answer all of these deep painful cries that I have been stuck under. No thank you. Instead, I'd prefer to make it on my own and find my Identity from sources like my job, my kids, my status, and my wife. In the process I'll end up sabotaging them all and creating more pain for myself. But this is what I choose."

Ridiculous, right? This is what the people of Judah did before their exile, which is where we jumped into the story with Nehemiah. And this is what you and I have done. For many of us Christian men, the primary "broken cistern" we've been using is our wife. Since we haven't been seeking to carry God's image, we've begun working to carry our wife's image. We've begun making ourselves into the version of a man that we think would satisfy her, and in the process we've lost our individual personhood. We've lost our other-ness. We've lost the unique and powerful man that God made us to be.

Make no mistake, friend, when you don't understand the full weight, the full importance, the full mind-shattering newness of the fact that you were created in God's image, you absolutely will look to be defined by something or someone else. And none of it will fuel you long term. None of it will establish you. None of it will end the questions. Everything other than Jesus will always leave you needing more.

So, welcome, Man of Identity. Welcome to your resurrection, your revival, your new birth. Now is the time. Wake up and realize that you've been using your wife, to meet your primal need for Identity and belonging—a need that only God can and should meet. Wake up and repent of making her your idol and neglecting the true lover of your soul, Jesus your king.

YOUR FATHER'S SON

And if you're looking for your Identity from something else—work, success, money, kids, friends, video games, sports, church, ministry—you may excel at those things for a time. But you know that they won't meet your need to belong and to be settled in your soul. You already feel this is true. You can't shake that nagging insecurity. Your confidence is hanging by the thread of your performance.

If for some reason things go wrong—maybe all of a sudden you don't have all the money that you thought you did. Maybe your kids go haywire on you. Maybe your ministry falters . All of a sudden you discover that you have no inner, unshakeable assuredness. You're scared. This is why you must be anchored, the way God anchored Adam in the beginning: "Man, you are like me, the God of creation. You look like me. You represent me. You are in my family. I am your Dad."

Identity.

In his classic life-transforming book, *Wild at Heart*, John Eldredge makes the point that a man's central question in life is, "Do I have what it takes?" And it's true. We are all wondering if we have what it takes to do something meaningful with the time we've been given. But my goal for you is that you stop wondering and that you learn the answer. That it begins to flow through you like rushing water. And you walk in it.

"Do I have what it takes?"

If we don't find our answer to this question in a source that is immovable, and healthy, then we are the city of Jerusalem whose walls were utterly destroyed. We are vulnerable and open to attack. We are weak and easily offended. Simple disagreements at home are not just a temporary clash where we work it out and get past it. Instead, they become enduring attacks on our insecure core. Instead of hearing our wife's heart and being able to work towards healing, all we hear is, "No, I don't have what it takes."

A reprimand from your supervisor at work, even if it is completely well-meaning and respectful, sinks talons into your soul and whispers to you, "You do not have what it takes."

An urgent financial need, the car breaking down, puts you in a tight money situation, and rather than responding in power and grit and leading your family through the crisis, you take it personally. You feel down on yourself for not being a better provider and a better man, or even a real man at all who would clearly be able to fix his own car. Your tiny bank account and your broken down car are blaring at you, "You don't have what it takes."

But God says differently. He declared over Adam that man is to have dominion over all of creation and to be fruitful and multiply. This is him saying, "Listen. I trust you. I, God, the perfect and powerful Almighty—I trust you, little man that I just whipped up out of the dirt of the ground. Yeah, you're small and made of dirt, but don't ever let yourself think that you are not worthy or valuable. I could just as easily say to myself, 'I'm going to rule and take dominion over this earth. And I'll handle it myself because I know better than anyone what is right and good. But I choose to trust you to take care of it on my behalf. It's mine, and I value it. But I'm handing it over to you because I think you can handle it. And I love you. I see myself in you, and that makes me proud of you—proud to be your Dad."

Isn't this what we all want from our dads? To be trusted? To be told, even in the face of everything going wrong in our lives, "You have what it takes?" This is exactly how God is establishing you. He says that this really is who you are. And you are good. You are so good, in fact, that he challenges you to go. Run. Be fruitful over the whole earth. Don't hold back. You were meant to be every bit of yourself, fully unrestrained and without hesitation.

YOUR REDEMPTION

If we men find ourselves overrun by whatever aspect of our world carries too much sway over us—be it baseball, or money, or health, or parenting, or marriage—then we are not living in the fullness of our Identity. For Men of Identity, nothing has power over us because we are established in Jesus. Consequently, we are able to live in an outward fashion, offering strength and love and value to our world, rather than living with our focus inward and afraid of the next threatening source of pain.

Jesus is holding out his hand, and he's inviting you: "Will you receive what I have for you? Forgiveness is the removal of your sin and shame and self-doubt. What is left in you is gold that I created in the beginning. Heaven is here for you now.

Find your Identity here, in the redemption of Jesus.

***

Chapter Notes

1) "Definition of IDENTITY." Accessed October 16, 2019. https://www.merriam-webster.com/dictionary/identity.

2) "Edwin Louis Cole Quote: Being a Male Is a Matter of Birth. Being a..." Accessed November 4, 2019. https://www.azquotes.com/quote/751497.

2

GOD'S OPINION, YOUR REALITY

IN ONE OF my favorite passages in all of Scripture, Judges chapter six, God's people, the Israelites, had begun to stray from the Lord. They once again "did what was evil" (vs. 1) in his sight, and consequently were given over into the hands of a foreign people: the Midianites. They had forgotten who they were, a people chosen by and set apart for God. So they lived according to their own wants and ways and effectively removed themselves from experiencing his covenant blessings of prosperity and protection.

It was so bad that they began making hiding places for both themselves and their provisions in the caves of the mountains. They had to struggle to survive, since, as soon as the Israelites planted their crops, the Midianites would gather their allies and literally devour the land, leaving nothing behind. The Scripture actually says the land was getting "laid waste" (vs. 5) and that Israel was "brought very low" (vs. 6) because of this.

Can you imagine having every single one of your efforts to provide and bring increase, to steward your life, be completely destroyed each time you try? Maybe you actually can imagine it. Maybe you don't have to imagine because you are actually living it. You feel like you're spinning your wheels constantly and are never actually moving forward. Jesus is letting you down. Your life is going nowhere and you can't figure out why. All you know is that your life is perpetually stolen out from under you every step of the way.

In this place of utter desperation, Judges chapter six says that God's people cried out to him.

What about you? Will you cry out to him in a new way? Will you stop crying, "God, what are you doing?! God, can't you see me?! God, I'm dying here!"

Instead will you humble yourself? Will you cry out, "God, I'm a desperate man! God, I'm undone! God, I need you! Take me and make me more into your image! God, save me, I'm drowning."

GIDEON ENTERS THE SCENE

After the people of Israel were brought to their place of repentance where they were finally willing to hear God's heart, he brought along a single man named Gideon. Verse eleven reads,

> The angel of the LORD came and sat under the terebinth tree at Ophrah, which belonged to Joash the Abiezrite, while his son Gideon was beating out wheat in the winepress to hide it from the Midianites.

This man, Gideon, decided to fulfill his duty of threshing wheat in the wrong place with the wrong tools. He should have been on the threshing floor, which would have been elevated, exposed, and open to the wind. Instead, in order to hide himself and his crop, he was processing the wheat inside the hidden, more enclosed and protective, shelter of a winepress. We can see this in one of two ways. One possibility is that Gideon is being brave and courageous and shrewd, as he was at least finding a way to carry on with his job of survival amidst this pillaging from his enemies. He was forming a resistance against the enemies of God.

That's possible. And maybe there was some of that going on in him.

But it's actually quite likely that he was afraid. Rather than believing that God would be with him to protect and provide for him, he had to take matters into his own hands to secure himself. So he went into hiding to do a basic daily chore. If you read further into the chapter, you'll see it stated clearly that Gideon was afraid of going after the first mission God gave him, and so he performed it at night under the cover of dark. It is likely that this fearfulness was showing itself in Gideon here as well.

YOU ARE MORE THAN GIDEON

Whatever the case, a man who, unlike Gideon, finds his Identity and affirmation in what the Father thinks of him has zero need to hide. You must learn to live this way. What God has declared over you about who you are and how much you are worth is more true than any threat that comes against you, no matter what it is and no matter where it comes from. So, as a man of Identity you can, even under the heaviest attack imaginable, stand up in the sight of all your enemies. You can live in such a way that nothing derails you from your course because God alone determines your destiny.

When you begin to hide in fear, you actually empower the very thing that you are afraid of, and you give it the authority to determine your destiny. Fear empowers evil. Fear empowers pain, hurt, and bitterness. Fear empowers strife and disease. Fear is what moves people to stop seeking God, to stop serving and living for God, and to start finding other lesser gods. And if you are familiar at all with the Old Testament, then you know that once you engage in finding other gods to meet your needs, you are on a quick path toward complete life-collapse.

GIDEON'S CALL, YOUR EMPOWERMENT

Back to Gideon.

He's hiding in the winepress, and the Angel of the LORD walks in and says,

> "The LORD is with you, O mighty man of valor." (Judges 6:12)

Do you get this? As Gideon was empowering his physical and spiritual enemies by hiding in fear, God in mercy and grace and his indefatigable commitment to our good and our original created Identity, walks into Gideon's existence and calls him higher. In the middle of Gideon doing absolutely nothing to deserve a special visitation from Jesus, Jesus says to him, "I am with you. And guess what. You are actually mighty. You are valiant. You are the stuff that warriors and heroes are made of. Will you trust me? Will you trust that what I think of you is true?"

See, the very first thing out of God's mouth is affirming to him that he is not alone. He is not an orphan. He has not been abandoned. And not only that, God also assures Gideon that he is worth it. He is worth God's affirmation and commitment because he is not some weak little boy defined by fear. He is a mighty grown man full of valor and nobility and honor and strength.

This is how God calls *you*. In the middle of your fear and living small. In the middle of your cowering. God calls you. When, in the eyes of everyone around you—men, women, your family, your wife, your boss, your church— you are not living in valor, God sees who you really are. And he doesn't care one bit about how you appear on the outside. God's esteem for you is not rooted in your behavior. His esteem for you is rooted in his original vision, the vision he had when he first conceived of you before he ever touched paintbrush to canvas.

Your Identity is not equivalent to your behavior. Your Identity is instead who God made you to be outside of your behavior in any given moment. If you begin living in your Identity, then yes, it spills out into your behavior, and your actions begin to match with who God made you to be. Now you're living in authenticity and integrity.

But the reverse is not true. Your behavior does not spill over into your Identity. Your Identity stands unchanged, though it may be marred by your sin and the attack from your enemies.

YOUR IDENTITY, THE KEY TO LIFE-CHANGE

In this story in Judges, God's vision for Gideon was that he was a mighty man of valor. But we have zero evidence that Gideon has ever done anything valiant up to this point in his life.

So what we have here is a beautiful and mind-blowing truth: God's fixation upon Gideon's true Identity as his mighty warrior was in itself the catalyst for

Gideon's massive transformation. This Identity being spoken into the fabric of Gideon's soul was the spark that ignited his strong warrior-heart to come alive. And consequently Gideon was propelled into his destiny to be a savior of God's people.

The truth is that your Identity comes before your actions, but we usually have it completely wrong. When we feel down on ourselves for not living up to the standards that we know we should be meeting, we consequently dismiss any notion that we are a valuable child of God. Maybe we sometimes accept the child of God part, but the valuable part? No. That's highly doubtful. We feel like arrogant hypocrites when we even begin to consider that maybe we have something good to offer the world because our past doesn't reflect this. Or our past **and** present don't reflect this.

But when we go here in our minds we are calling God a liar and we are refusing his Identity for us. In so doing, we separate ourselves from the very remedy that would bring both the heart transformation and the life transformation that we so desperately want. Do you want change? Then humble yourself and believe God. Believe him more than your regret, more than your guilt, more than your list of mistakes and wrongs. Jesus cancelled

> the record of debt that stood against us with its legal demands. This he set aside, nailing it to the cross. (Colossians 2: 14)

LEAVING BITTERNESS BEHIND

Gideon had to learn this lesson as well. His immediate response to God's too-good-to-be-true Identity for him was to doubt and question. He responded with all of the reasons why what God was saying couldn't possibly be true. All of the evidence was stacked against this Identity that was being spoken from God's mouth.

> "Please sir, if the LORD is with us, why then has all this happened to us? And where are all his wonderful deeds that our fathers recounted to us, saying, 'Did not the LORD bring us up from Egypt?' But now the LORD has forsaken us and given us into the hand of Midian." (Judges 6:13)

His response is further evidence that Gideon was in this winepress not out of some kind of secret resilient hope, but in near resignation and even bitterness.

Be honest with yourself. Are you bitter, discouraged, and hopeless? Are you running out of drive because you've been stuck? After all of your all-consuming efforts to fight through, have the enemies in your life not even budged? No matter how hard you've worked and no matter how much wheat you have threshed in your hiding places, just trying to get by, you feel like your enemies are still waiting to ravage you.

So you've argued with God, "God, you're not with me like you said you would be! Where the heck are you? Where are all the wonderful works you used to do? You know, the ones everybody talks about. Everyone says you are there and that you're real. Everyone says that you speak and you change their lives. But where are you for me? You've forsaken me even though you said you wouldn't."

When your Identity is not settled in rock solid assurance, then the circumstances that you face can easily steal it away. And they can bring death inside of you, causing you to decay into this dark soup of despair and hurt. This is exactly where satan wants you, because from this place a joyful and victorious life is impossible. You will have no chance of bringing value to the world and seeing God's kingdom take shape around you while you are stuck in bitterness and hopelessness. When your Identity isn't settled, then you whore yourself out to the highest bidding emotion or circumstance that comes your way.

Harsh, I know. But real.

MY HEALTH JOURNEY

When I was twenty years old, I started to develop the debilitating health issue that has been a battle of mine and my wife's now for nearly thirteen years. It began at a time when I was making some poor decisions and had been, in certain ways, walking out of the fathering of the Lord. Not that I was leaving him behind and jumping headlong into a life of sin and debauchery, but I was elevating other lesser gods above him.

It was during this time, which also happened to be our engagement year, that this disease took hold in my body. It became serious very quickly. Arthritis spread from one ankle to all of my major joints: ankles, knees, hips, spine, elbows, shoulders, wrists, jaw. Everywhere. And while my joints were swelling my weight was dropping. Between my proposal to my wife and our actual wedding day, I dropped almost twenty pounds.

My body was under an all-out attack. I was losing weight, losing mobility, losing use of my hands, walking with a limp, and growing more and more tired. Before, I had been very athletic: exercising regularly, working a landscaping job, hiking in the mountains, becoming that famous pro ballplayer/evangelist.

As I mentioned, I had been looking to sources outside the heart of my Father for my belonging and worth. Because I had been in this place where my Identity was already under attack due to my own poor choices, the sickness started to take me out emotionally and spiritually as well as physically. For nearly a decade, I plummeted into self-pity. As if mimicking my body's inability to wake up and rise out of bed, my spirit wasn't waking and rising to the occasion each day. I wasn't fighting forward in faith toward victory.

If you think your situation is too difficult for you and too far gone for God to reach in and rescue you, then I challenge you to contact me. I am not being arrogant here or starting a "mine is worse than yours" battle. But I'm calling you higher. I'm inviting you to drop your self-pity. You need to hear this.

I've been bedridden off and on through my 20s and 30s, the so-called prime of life. I was despairing of life itself (2 Corinthians 1:8). When my weight dropped to just above 100 pounds, and I had to pee in a jug because I couldn't make it to the bathroom in the middle of the night, my wife thought I was literally going to die. But I am very much alive. The battle is very far from being lost. You too can stand up one more time and jump back in. Don't give in to the self-pity that says, "I'm just that screwed up. There is no hope for me." You cannot let whatever comes against you have the power to determine who you will be. The only one who has that authority is your Creator.

When I was at my lowest in this sickness, and I was locked in my depression, I started to search the Bible for whatever God had to say about sickness and healing. I wasn't looking for my Identity necessarily. I was just looking for some semblance of hope, no matter how small a fragment it might be. I had been taught and had absorbed through osmosis in our modern Christian culture that if I was sick and not getting better, then it must be God's will. (Side note: Circumstance should never decide God's will. God's will always decides circumstance.)

That belief system, for me, was about as useful as garbage. It led me into deeper discouragement and depression. I began to wonder, what kind of Father would want to torture me like this? What kind of father would willingly inflict this hell on me when Jesus died to save me from hell?

So, in the midst of being bedridden and unable to climb stairs—unable to hug my wife, hold my daughter, and just be a man—I threw out everything I had "known" about healing and sickness. I had to know for myself, not from what anyone else had taught, what I was going to believe. Does God heal? If he does heal, does he heal everyone? Is it his will to heal me? Is it NOT his will to heal me? Does he have a different plan that involves me being sick?

As I searched the Bible with fresh eyes, throwing away all of my pre-existing beliefs about God and sickness, I found that God not only **can** heal, but also **wants** to heal. It is his will to heal. He showed me promise after promise that spurred me on to pursue him for total and miraculous health in my body. God heals all our diseases according to Psalm 103. Jesus bore our sicknesses and carried our pains according to Isaiah 53. I started to say to myself, "Wait a minute! If I'm going to be a Christian and follow Jesus, then I had better do it all the way. I'd better believe everything I see in this book and not come up with my own explanations that help me feel better about wherever my life is lacking his Kingdom power. I'd better not pick and choose which pieces I'll embrace.

"I'm not going to be a divided man with divided beliefs. So even though I am in the middle of sickness right now, the Bible says that I shouldn't be. It also says that sickness is not actually any part of me. So this thing in my body is illegal. I am actually—truly—a vibrant and alive man of God."

I discovered that sickness was not my Identity. This dark circumstance that was trying to latch onto me and whisper into my ear what my destiny would be actually had no part in my true Identity as a child of God.

Slowly, I stopped being bedridden, and in order to actually live out my beliefs, I started praying for people to be healed. I wouldn't just add them to my list of people to pray for as I thought of them throughout the week. I would actually encounter people, strangers and friends alike, in my daily life who needed healing right there, in the moment. So I would pray for them right where we were, putting Jesus on the spot to either come through with a healing or not.

Now, I have many stories of miraculous healings, which are the topic of another book. But the point for us right now is that I started living in a way where my actions and experience lined up with what I had newly learned my Identity to be, which was a man of health made whole by Jesus. The Identity, drawn from God's heart, precluded my experience. Transformation began in my belief about who I was and worked its way out from there.

I adopted the attitude of, "You know what, satan? You can do whatever you're going to do to come against me, but I am going to march forward in my Identity of health and healing. If my body doesn't start to experience it right now, it's not going to stop me. I'm going to do everything I can to bring the healing to others, anyway."

How do *you* need to take action right now? How do you need to step out in faith and affirm your true Identity? Or maybe it's too soon for you to even answer that question. Maybe you need to instead ask, "What *is* my Identity?"

IT DOESN'T MATTER HOW YOU FEEL

God will meet you when you ask, no matter where you are, even if you are still in frustrated defeat. As we've seen, Gideon responded to God's initial call in despair and bitterness. But watch what God does.

> And the LORD turned to him and said, "Go in this might of yours and save Israel from the hand of Midian; do not I send you?" (Judges 6:14)

God is frustratingly irrational at times. He has identified Gideon as a mighty man of valor in spite of his fearful cowering. Gideon responds with doubt, accusation and bitterness, and God completely ignores him. But rather than engage Gideon's despair and validate that thinking, God stays his course. He acts as if Gideon had never said a word and speaks to him as if he were a completely different man than the one we see.

And you know what? You are a completely different man. God says to you, "Go in this might of **yours**." You might question, what might? What valor? There's no evidence of it. But God sees something in you that maybe even no one else can see. He sees who you can and will be. He sees your destiny as he decreed it, not as your circumstances are trying to determine.

You might not feel mighty and powerful. And you might feel like a piece of garbage. But it's simply not true. It's time for you to take on a new Identity. Not the Identity that your wife says over you. Not the Identity that the thoughts in your mind say over you. Not the Identity that your health or your performance at work or your social status say over you. Not what your business success and money accumulation say over you.

Instead, take on what God says over you, the ancient Identity that he settled before you were created and that he sealed eternally with his blood poured over you.

WHOSE VOICE WILL YOU CHOOSE?

Gideon goes on in verse 15 of Judges chapter six, still in his unbelief, and he questions,

> "Please, Lord, how can I save Israel? Behold, my clan is the weakest in Manasseh, and I am the least in my father's house."

In this whole tribe, this whole nation, I am the weakest and the least.

This is his true self assessment, his true self worth, showing. And God's words were coming into direct conflict with the narrative that Gideon had been living under. The self doubt and the lack of confidence that you experience in your life is nothing new. It's ancient. We see it here and we can see it back even before Gideon. Since the beginning of humanity, we men have failed to take ownership of ourselves and our identities. We have wallowed in our excuses and our delusions of worthlessness even as far back as Moses when God visited him on Mount Sinai.

He questioned God, "Who am I? I'm the wrong guy, Lord. I can't even speak. How am I going to confront Pharaoh people free?

Go back to Adam, who, once he sinned and ate the fruit, doesn't even take ownership. He avoids blame and again makes excuses, saying that the woman God gave him made him do it.

This ancient propensity to not take ownership of our actions and our identities has poisoned our lives. We distance ourselves from our self. We are not proud to be us, especially when we mess up. We don't walk in security and the certainty of our basic life-competence. We find excuses to discredit and doubt and look down on ourselves. And then we blame everything else for our pain and lack of progress in life.

But this propensity in you is not the fault of anything or anyone else in your life right now. It's not even the fault of the voices that have told you all of the wounding lies about your Identity. You, my friend, are the one who has chosen to agree with them. You have chosen which voices you will give more credence to. You have let down the defenses of your mind and your heart and have allowed satan's arrows to lodge and inject their poison inside.

Now, however, you have the opportunity to choose a new path. Will you rise to the occasion and choose to agree with God? He's inviting you. He says, "I will be with you. You might be the least and the weakest, and you might not have much to show for yourself, but I will be with you and I am a warrior. I am a champion.

"I'm not asking you to go forward and conquer in your own power and strength. I want you to go forward knowing me, tapping into my strength in you. You are always meant to live from me as your life-source anyway."

WHEN INADEQUACY RULES

Just as he spoke all of this over Gideon before he had ever done anything noteworthy, so also, in the book of Genesis, God gave us men our Identity before we had done anything to warrant it. He declared us to be in his image and to have dominion over his creation and to not cower in fear—to not hide in our winepresses—from the outset, so that he could be the one to set the tone for us. Because if God our Father is not setting the tone for our lives, then our fear of being inadequate will. We will tiptoe around, being nice above all else, so as not to expose ourselves to anyone's disapproval. Because, for our fragile or non-existent identities, disapproval is like a death sentence.

You may have heard of the "nice guy syndrome" that was made popular by the ground-breaking book, *No More Mr. Nice Guy*, by Robert Glover. The message of the book is that there are too many nice guys walking the earth right now. Too many men who let what other people think about them determine who they will be. Too many men who don't know their identities. So they let themselves be defined by passing opinions in hopes of finding fulfillment in the approval of others.

I'm sorry to say, this is you. This is me. We have done this. And it's time we stop. It is sinful and unholy. It is not like our Father, and it is feeding the proliferation of evil in our world. When we men let ourselves be defined by the enemies that come against us or the opinions of our friends, bosses, wives, and children, we sink into the dregs of apathy and self-pity. We no longer exalt Jesus and proudly run after him for the world to see. We instead apologetically shift along from day to day hoping not to rock the boat. But the kingdom suffers violence, according to Jesus. And violent—literally, strong and forceful—men take it by force.

> From the days of John the Baptist until now the kingdom of heaven has suffered violence, and the violent take it by force. (Matthew 11:12)

In other words, kingdom men absolutely do rock the boat. Not in anger or self-righteous revenge or arrogance. But somehow, in love and compassion and joy, our aggression coexists and we make people uncomfortable. This flies in the face of the prevailing Christian notion that true Christians are called to be polite all the time and that somehow ruffling feathers is against God's heart.

Again, we do not have license to be harmful jerks. But we need to start living unshaken by the opinion of others. God's opinion is the only one that truly matters. So we need to settle for ourselves whether or not we will believe what he says.

3

WELCOME TO...YOU

AS I QUIETLY sat in on my dad's meetings with his clients, watching him examine the dog with the infected wound, or the cat with a foxtail stuck in her eye, I knew that I was welcome. I had no expert knowledge or training with which to offer my services. I received no paycheck to prove that I was a valuable contributing member of the animal hospital crew. And as a seven year old kid, I certainly didn't have the height with which to be able to look my dad or his staff square in the eye. I was just a kid who loved my dad, who loved the animals, and who loved being there.

And that was enough.

As my dad's son, I didn't have to always be working as long as I was on the clock. I didn't have to "have a good reason" for being in any certain part of the hospital. I could spend hours in my dad's office, at his desk, amidst all his papers. I could explore the closet where other work clothes and smocks would hang. I could venture behind the front desk, into the exam rooms, out into the back with all the dogs. I was even welcome to waltz into the surgery room when Dad was in the middle of an operation. I even remember one time watching him operate on a dog that had a maggot infestation. Absolutely disgusting, but also weirdly fascinating.

Everyone there knew me and knew I was free to roam. If they ever had a problem with me (which they didn't), they knew to take it up with my dad. And they knew if they gave me problems (which they didn't), they knew my dad would take it up with **them**. These were the joys of being my dad's son, given a place of honor, freedom, belonging, and even authority in his domain. Or, in other words, his kingdom.

Years later, as a fledgling adult fresh out of high school, I walked into my dad's new hospital. He had, in time, relocated to a new town, new practice, completely new staff. The place was completely unknown to me, and I to them. But after several years of he and I not seeing each other, I decided to visit, and the only place I knew to find him was at his hospital down the street from my soon-to-be first college apartment.

As I walked in and introduced myself, "Hi, I'm Ken's son," it was clear: I was welcome. The receptionist stopped her work to find my dad. I was invited back into the staff-only work room where the cages of just-as-friendly cats were, and my dad stopped what he was doing for me. He stopped his day to take me to lunch.

I was his son. I was honored. I was free. I belonged. I had authority.

WHAT YOUR IDENTITY MEANS FOR YOU

It's true that, in God's Kingdom, you and I are many things. We are warriors. We are kings. We are men who love others and men who face resistance. We are apostles, prophets, pastors, teachers, evangelists, and servants. We are prayer champions and advocates of the weak. We are teachers, policemen, farmers, engineers, managers, and waiters. And while all these deserve their own attention, they are not of the same primary importance as our identity as sons.

Sonship exists prior to any other label we take on in our lives. Even before we step into our biblical roles as kings, priests, and the bride of Christ, we exist as sons. In the natural world, being a son involves no action or decision on our part. It involves absolutely zero earning. It just is. So also, in the spiritual, in

God's Kingdom, our sonship just is. And it is the core, the epicenter, from which everything else radiates in earth-shaking power.

And it is our sonship that makes our honor, freedom, power, and authority even possible. Because we are sons, we are free to roam our Dad's halls with confidence and boldness. As the book of Hebrews tells us, we can come boldly before our Father's throne any time we need anything. We do not tiptoe around gingerly.

The fact that you are a son of God, completely accepted and honored, needs to start influencing how you conduct yourself every single day, with every single person, in every single arena. This starts with yourself and how you think about you. It radiates out to your wife, how you treat her and think of her and how you think of yourself as a husband. From there it reaches into your parenting and who you are as a dad. And of course, the entire rest of the world also gets to benefit from you stepping into your full Identity as a son who is connected with the Father and who is bringing his presence to earth. As Romans chapter eight says,

> For the creation waits with eager longing for the revealing of the sons of God.

Creation itself is waiting, almost painfully, for us to understand this. Because creation knows that, when we do, the tides of history will shift toward our Creator, and all of existence, including the rocks that cry out in praise, will reap the benefits. So this sonship Identity absolutely must engulf our DNA and flow through our veins to the extent that it carries the nourishing truth of who we are into every corner of our body, soul, and spirit. We need to both invite the Holy Spirit to implant it in our thinking and also proactively choose it by taking action to align our thoughts with it. We want to be hearers of the word, receiving openly the supernatural transformation of Jesus. And we want to be doers of the word, men who act on what we've received, putting it into practice and sinking it into the soil of our being so that it actually does something to us and produces the benefit we are hoping for.

* * *

> "Everyone then who hears these words of mine and does them will be like a wise man who built his house on the rock." (Matthew 7:24)

And in this choice to embrace Jesus's truth, we thereby declare our allegiance to our King:

> "If you love me, you will keep my commandments." (John 14:15)

"OKAY, BUT WHAT IS MY IDENTITY?"

By now, three chapters and an introduction into the book, you may be wondering what exactly is your Identity. Yes, you understand this idea of being God's son, of carrying his image, of being your own man independent of your woman or anyone else. But practically, in a rubber-meets-the-road fashion, what does this look like?

Every man has to walk this path of discovery for himself. And he cannot simply conjure up his Identity from a selection of appealing characteristics or truths. He can't rely only on surveying other men, past and present, and pulling his favorite snippets from each. This is what some men may do in the world, but not you and I. You and I do not walk this independent of God walking through the "garden" with us, as he did with Adam. Consequently, you and I discover our Identity through a process of seeking and revealing. We seek God's heart, and he brings revelation. We ingest the revelation and grow hungry for more. So we seek again. And in our seeking we present to him our own questions, observations, opinions, and desires. "God will you make me this way? Will you transform that part of me? Is this particular quality of 'manliness' one that is truly consistent with your heart?"

That said, I don't want to leave you completely alone in discovering what practical pieces make up your Identity, so I am going to share with you some truths that I have learned about my Identity as a man in the Kingdom. Some of them, you will see, are clearly more "spiritual," and having to do with Bible-y, Christian-y things. Others are more practical, like the way a man relates to others, the way he views money, or the way he treats his family. But in reality they are all both practical and spiritual, and if you find yourself compartmentalizing between Jesus and real life, then you've got some work to do. And that's a topic for another book.

I've done my best to choose certain pieces of my Identity that are most likely to surprise you, offend you, slap you in the face, and wake you up to the idea that maybe we haven't been taught the whole story. Maybe it's time for us to venture out into the wilderness for ourselves so we can hear real truth straight from the mouth of Jesus himself.

Here we go.

A RIGHTEOUS SAINT

I cannot stand the phrase, "I'm just a sinner saved by grace." This has become a mantra of the church in our culture, and it promotes self-degradation, depression, and the belief that I am constantly screwing up. A man who sees himself this way does not see himself as being able to offer value to the world. Instead, he's probably sinning right now without even knowing it, and if it weren't for the reluctant, begrudging grace of God, he would be thrown immediately into hell in order to spare the rest of us from the stench of his presence. Think, "Sinners in the Hands of an Angry God," the widely read sermon by Jonathan Edwards. While we have rightly taught the reality of sin and the need for redemption, we have mistakenly begun to hate ourselves as disgusting sinners, even after being redeemed.

Instead, you sir, are a righteous saint. You were a sinner, yes. But Jesus lifted you from the mud and dark sin that was engulfing you and sucking the life from you. He vanquished those enemies and threw them so far away that he cannot call them to remembrance. He found you worth such a high price that only his blood would match the price tag for your life. You are cherished, honored, worthy.

> Because you are precious in my eyes, and honored, and I love you, I give men in return for you, peoples in exchange for your life. (Isaiah 43:4)
> But you are a chosen race, a royal priesthood, a holy nation, a people for his own possession, that you may proclaim the excellencies of him who called you out of darkness into his marvelous light. (1 Peter 2:9)

* * *

LIKE JESUS, FULL OF GLORY, AUTHORITY, AND POWER

That subtitle probably offends some.

How can I be like Jesus? How can you say that I have authority and glory just like he does? No way!

I know. The words of the Bible are offensive. They challenge the religious crap in us. They make us want to pridefully scream, "No!" when what Jesus wants is for us to humbly say, "Yes." Like when he told John the Baptist to baptize him, though John protested. Or when he told Peter to let him wash his feet, though Peter hated the thought. We cry out, "Not so, Lord! May it never be that I am exalted in that way!"

And yet, as offensive as it is to our religious dispositions, Jesus himself says that he has actually given us his glory:

> "The glory that you have given me I have given to them." (John 17:22)

He also tells us that he has given us his authority to implement his will and domain in the earth:

> "Behold, I have given you authority to tread on serpents and scorpions, and over all the power of the enemy, and nothing shall hurt you." (Luke 10:19)

The book of Romans elaborates on this authority that Jesus has given us, even going so far as to assert that we are to "reign as kings" in this life:

> For if because of one man's trespass (lapse, offense) death reigned through that one, much more surely will those who receive [God's] overflowing grace (unmerited favor) and the free gift of righteousness [putting them into right standing with Himself] reign as kings in life through the one Man Jesus Christ (the Messiah, the Anointed One). (Romans 5:17 AMPC)

I have chosen to get off my prideful religious butt that says, "Not so, Lord, I'm not glorious or authoritative." I have chosen to agree with him, instead, and to see where that takes me. So far, it's taken me deeper into love with him, humility before others, and a richer, fuller life. I love better. I speak truer. I feel happier.

Then there's the question of power. I have power as well. Not originating from me, because, remember, my DNA itself came from my Father. But the power is mine nonetheless, through faith. Jesus is telling us men, like he told his disciples, "You give them something to eat. You heal the sick. You raise the dead and cleanse lepers. You unleash or withhold forgiveness. You curse or bless. It's in your hands." As much as we'd like to argue this, resist it, and tell Jesus that he's wrong, we can't escape the fact that the gospels are bursting with verse after verse along these lines, but I'll give you two.

> "For truly, I say to you, if you have faith like a grain of mustard seed, you will say to this mountain, 'Move from here to there,' and it will move, and nothing will be impossible for you." (Matthew 17:20)
> "And these signs will accompany those who believe: in my name they will cast out demons; they will speak in new tongues; 18 they will pick up serpents with their hands; and if they drink any deadly poison, it will not hurt them; they will lay their hands on the sick, and they will recover." (Mark 16:17-18)

I HAVE A RIGHT TO HEALTH

According to the accurate Hebrew meaning of Isaiah 53—which is perhaps the most famous "Atonement" passage in the Bible, where the full implication of Jesus's work is set forth—Jesus not only took on our sins and trespasses, but he also carried our sicknesses and pains. Verses 4 and 5 read:

Surely he has borne our griefs
    and carried our sorrows;
  yet we esteemed him stricken,
    smitten by God, and afflicted.
  But he was pierced for our transgressions;
    he was crushed for our iniquities;
  upon him was the chastisement that brought us peace,

and with his wounds we are healed.

According to Strong's Hebrew dictionary, the word that we translated into "griefs" is the Hebrew word *choli*, which means "sickness."[1] In fact, every other time this word appears, it is translated in some way that refers to physical disease. Also, the word that we translated as "sorrows" is the Hebrew word *makob*, which means physical and mental pain.[2]

Unlike our modern translations of this verse, Matthew's gospel actually gets it right. Matthew chapter eight reads:

> That evening they brought to him many who were oppressed by demons, and he cast out the spirits with a word and healed all who were sick. This was to fulfill what was spoken by the prophet Isaiah: "He took our illnesses and bore our diseases." (Matthew 8:16-17)

Our bodies were bought with the blood of Jesus along with our spirits. Psalm 103 seems to assign a parallel importance to both sin and sickness:

Bless the Lord, O my soul,
> and forget not all his benefits,

who forgives all your iniquity,
> who heals all your diseases. (Psalm 103:2-3)

Our emotional struggles and our sins, quite honestly, can be somewhat intangible and vague. So the common, but inaccurate, understanding of this verse allows us to accept a less than powerful experience of the work of Jesus. We can continue in defeated struggle and have this wispy notion that somehow Jesus has taken care of it. But when we see his atonement as including our physical bodies, as ridding us of disease, now all of a sudden we are forced to reckon with the fact that we either are or are not ***actually*** experiencing the reality of the gospel.

And so, we are forced to address the question of our Identity. It's time to stop settling for nice-sounding beliefs about what Jesus has done, when those beliefs aren't resulting in an actual readout. It's time for us to enter into such a faith, such a relationship with God, that what he says to be true actually becomes true in our experience. If our Identity is as sons of God, then we need to live like it. I therefore will push for complete health. I will not settle for less. This is my Identity according to the word of my Father, just as much as righteousness and authority and glory.

I AM DESIGNED TO PROSPER

God promised his people in Deuteronomy that they would prosper if they remained in covenant with him. He said that they would be the head and not the tail. He also gave them the power to create wealth. In the Psalms he says that he makes the work of our hands to prosper. And in the gospels Jesus assures us that our Father will provide everything for us. We no longer need to worry or panic like others, because every need is met. Like the father in the prodigal son story, everything that God has is ours.

I AM FREE AND VICTORIOUS

It's time for you to stop letting yourself be defined by your sins, even your addictions. It's only satan who wants you to take on the Identity of sinner, of addict, of one who keeps circling the same mountain over and over again. I don't care if you've only been free and clear of a certain struggle since this morning, you speak over yourself the transforming grace of God that says you were set free. Believe in the truth. Do not believe in your performance.

MY UNIQUE IDENTITY AS A MAN

I could go on for a long time about different features of my spiritual Identity, but I want to also point out certain parts of who we get to be as men, men who make a difference in the world. Men who bring the things of God into the present tangible reality of our daily lives. So let me tell you about yourself.

You are emotionally strong. You do not need another human being to make you happy. You are able to find happiness and contentment even if you are alone. You do not need your wife to make you stable and at peace. You are stable regardless.

You do not quit. The world will throw every obstacle imaginable at you to derail you. And for too long your Christian brothers and forefathers have set a precedent of interpreting those obstacles as somehow indicative of God's will. "If something isn't working out, then don't push it, God wants something else." Don't believe it. You, as a man, take your directives from the mouth of God, and when life tries to shut you down, you shut it up by staying on the path, fighting forward, and refusing to surrender.

You bring value to your world. As a man of your home, you wake up each morning with the goal and privilege of giving love to your wife. You do not approach her from neediness, but from confident generosity and compassion. Instead of looking to receive from others, you look to give to them. You search for opportunities to make their lives better, knowing that your Father will see to it that your needs are met.

You rule over yourself and your space. You are not overrun by clutter and messiness. You bring order and you work and keep your home as Adam did.

You are not nice. You are not everyone's favorite. You are you, in all your glorious imperfections, fire, and opinions. You love, but you do not coddle. You are kind, but you are not subservient. You listen, but you also speak.

You are watchful, vigilant, a protector. You approach your day assuming that conflict will come. You embrace conflict as food for your growth, and rather than working to avoid it, you use it to serve you.

You do not let pain stop you. Pain only pushes you to get stronger and move farther. You have zero limits on you and you really are able to do anything. That is true. You can do literally anything.

You take God at face value. When he says, "You can do all things through Christ," you stop adding qualifiers and contextual explanations that dampen the roaring power of his voice. And you simply say, "Yes, Dad."

***

Chapter Notes

1) "Strong's Hebrew: 2483. חֳלִי (Choli) -- Sickness." Accessed December 6, 2019. https://biblehub.com/hebrew/2483.htm.

***

2) "Strong's Hebrew: 4341. מַכְאוֹב (Makob) -- Pain." Accessed December 6, 2019. https://biblehub.com/hebrew/4341.htm.

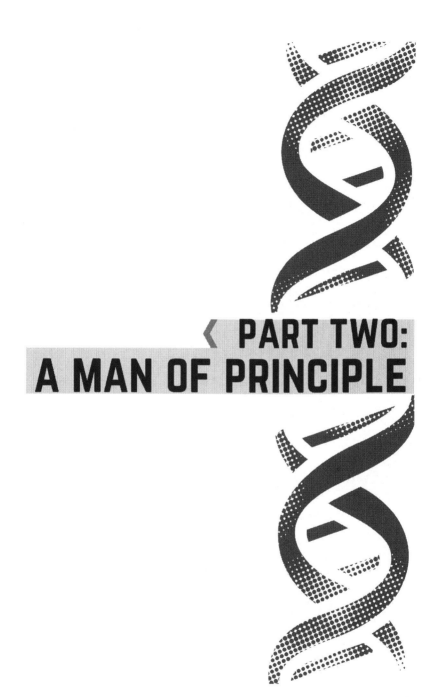

PART TWO:
A MAN OF PRINCIPLE

"A man's got to have a code, a creed to live by, no matter his job."

-*John Wayne*[3]

4

STOP PANDERING FOR APPROVAL

THERE WAS NO time. We had to hurry. Crawling on hands and knees through the two-foot-tall grass mingled with weeds, mingled with littered pinecones, I and my two brothers in arms had to keep advancing. We pushed our way through the thick undergrowth hoping beyond hope that no one would see us, least of all our enemies as they periodically drove by, making their rounds.

In a situation like this, a thousand thoughts race through your head. What if someone **does** see me? What if we are too late and our town is already lost? What if the grenades we're carrying in our packs accidentally go off as we're bumping and jostling our way up this steep slope in front of us?

"Another one's coming," Jeremiah whispered, indicating the enemy scout driving slowly toward us.

"Let's do it." Jeremiah's older, more reckless and dangerously overconfident brother, Caleb, had urged this whole mission in the first place.

Feeling out of my comfort zone and unsure of the wisdom of this plan, I complied. So together, the three of us—Jeremiah the youngest, Caleb his older brother, and I—reached into our packs, grabbed our weapon of choice, the mighty grenade, and let them fly. We sent them hurtling through the air toward the enemy who never saw them coming until it was too late. There was nothing she could do to stop them.

Suddenly, reality hit me and we were no longer three heroes sneaking behind enemy lines to save our village from destruction. We were three kids, out of school for the summer, living every young boy's dream of spending the summer outside in the woods, adventuring, and having nothing in the world to worry about except surviving our pretend "war" and making it back to "base" for lunch prepared for us by Jeremiah and Caleb's mom. And the grenades? Water balloons. The only threat they posed to us if they suddenly "went off" was the possibility of absolutely soaked shorts. Life was good. Until . . .

To this day, the three of us don't know whose water balloon actually made contact, but that didn't matter—not in that moment. In that moment immediately following the sounds of splashing water balloon on the hood of the passing car, the sudden application of the brakes to pull said car to a stop, and the angry opening and slamming of the driver's side door, nothing mattered anymore except the raw primal instinct to survive, at all costs. Even if it meant abandoning a brother in arms, leaving a man behind.

We had been innocuously water ballooning cars for nearly an hour by this point, never having the courage to actually make contact with our targets. The chances were good that none of the passing drivers had even noticed they were under attack, as our balloons usually barely even made it up the slope of the road-side gully in which we nestled. But this time, one of us found some of that inner strength, and it was more than we had prepared for.

As the driver stepped out of her car, yelling into the woods where we were now flawlessly executing our new battle plan of "run for your life at all costs," the manly, brotherly principles of nobility, honor, self-sacrifice, brotherhood, and owning up to your mistakes—they all vanished. We were no longer Men of Principle, guided by an honorable code of conduct. Instead, that code was overtaken by the urgency of the moment, the threat of certain death at the hands of Jeremiah and Caleb's mom, and subsequently *my* mom when she heard the news.

It was now "every man for himself," survival of the fittest, and it didn't matter who was lost in the scurry.

Unfortunately, this was very true, for Jeremiah, the youngest of the three of us, the youngest of his family of boys, and the one who often fought to keep up as we were out adventuring our summers away. This time, his less-developed speed cost him.

Caleb and I were flying through the woods, keeping in close proximity to each other the whole time. But not Jeremiah. The enemy scout was too fast for him. She "caught" him. When Caleb and I reached a safe distance away from the site of the crime, we confirmed what we had only suspected up to that point. Jeremiah was indeed "lost." The driver had gotten out, seen us, called after us, and Jeremiah was the only one—the youngest of us three—who was man enough to not run but to turn and take ownership for what we had done: water ballooning her car.

We later learned that this driver then escorted Jeremiah up the road a few houses to where he and Caleb and their family lived. Once there, she reported the whole incident to his mom. And Jeremiah faced the punishment that should have been all of ours. Meanwhile, Caleb and I knew better than to get caught, and we certainly knew better than to turn ourselves in by showing up back at the house too soon after the incident. So, after catching our breath and recovering from our flight to safety, we stayed outside, roaming through the wooded neighborhood as long as possible before finally having to return to fill our hungry stomachs.

As had been the case since that balloon's impact, we had no thoughts of Principle, of honor and integrity. We were merely having fun, avoiding getting caught, and consequently ignoring hunger. We were driven by our momentary needs and feelings, and we were more than happy to let Jeremiah deal with the fallout of our actions. Here's to you, Jeremiah. You were several years younger, but more man than me that day.

ANOTHER DNA BUILDING BLOCK: PRINCIPLE

Here we come to the second primal piece of a man's DNA: Principle. Before we carry the discussion any further, though, let's define what we mean by *Principle*. The term, as we will be using it, carries quite a distinct meaning from its plural form *principles*, and it's important that you and I understand each other and what role each of these words plays as we figure out how to be real men of the kingdom. The word *Principle* can be defined as:

> 1) a guiding sense of the requirements and obligations of right conduct[1]

Or:

> 2) a habitual devotion to right principles[2]

These definitions are what we will be meaning when we dive in to your becoming a Man of Principle. Just as you must become a Man of Identity, so you must become a Man of Principle. You must become a man who lives under the guiding sense of what good and right and honorable conduct should be. You must become a man who lives according to a "habitual devotion," that is, a persistent and unwavering clinging to your internal code that guides your thoughts, words, actions, and beliefs.

In other words, you must become a man who, unlike me on that fateful summer day, does not let your companion take the fall for a crime you equally committed. You must not let your primal drive for survival overtake your honor, your character, and your commitment to the heart of God.

In general, when we use the plural word, *principles*, any one of these definitions will carry the meaning we are looking for:

> 1) an accepted or professed rule of action or conduct
> 2) a fundamental, primary, or general law or truth from which others are derived
> 3) a fundamental doctrine or tenet; a distinctive ruling opinion
> 4) an adopted rule or method for application in action
> 5) a personal or specific basis of conduct or management[1]

A Man of Principle refers to a man who has chosen to live his life in the world and in God's kingdom by governing himself according to a certain code. That code, then, is comprised of principles, which are rules, tenets, or truths. And, to avoid all possible confusion, we'll use God's gift of capitalization: Principle for the one, and principle(s) for the other.

To be a Man of Principle, you will need both Principle and principles. One does not help you without the other. A man of Principle without a powerful guiding code to live by is a shallow man who loves the sound of living with honor and integrity but has done no work to actually bind himself to the higher authority of his God-inspired and self-instated code of conduct. A man who has a thorough understanding of a certain set of principles but who lacks the inner fire to live by his own powerful decision according to those principles is, during "good" times, legalistically obedient, trying to merely do the right thing and check all his boxes. Yuck! That kind of dead religious living with no heartfelt passion or fire is not at all what we're after. During "bad" times, it's no better. When the storms begin to pound him, he quickly becomes a deserter, a traitor who leaves the principles behind in search of some easier or more promising mode of living that will meet his urgent need to coddle his fear and comfort.

Both men are easily tossed when life gets difficult. Neither man is truly a Man of Principle, nor is he a Man of Identity. When a man is so unanchored and weak in the face of trouble, the lack of Principle is a sign of the deeper problem of still not having done the work of discovering who he is in the Kingdom, who he is in Jesus, who he is as a son of God.

PRINCIPLE STEMS FROM IDENTITY

Watch how closely linked Principle and Identity are with each other.

> The Lord God took the man and put him in the garden of Eden to work it and keep it. And the Lord God commanded the man, saying, "You may surely eat of every tree of the garden, but of the tree of the knowledge of good and evil you shall not eat, for in the day that you eat of it you shall surely die." (**Genesis 2:15-17**)

While you and I may not be worried about accidentally eating the wrong fruit and sending the whole course of history into a tailspin, we men face daily the challenge, and the privilege, of living as men of Principle by making powerful decisions about how we will conduct ourselves in this world. And in this portion of Genesis, God is offering to Adam that same manly privilege. He is asking, "What kind of man do you want to be, Adam? Don't let the world and situations that arise decide for you. You decide for yourself."

In this verse from Genesis, God lays down for Adam two simple principles by which to live. Principle number one: you can eat of any tree you want. Principle number two: except for this one. Done.

Not that difficult, right? Even though this is by no means the extensive code of conduct that we would expect from the holy Creator, it is enough. By establishing these principles, God is constructing an entity outside of Adam's feelings, which are prone to fickle fluctuation, that can govern his behavior. He doesn't force Adam into following the principles. He simply presents them before Adam to do with as he pleases. Would Adam choose to be a man of conviction who lives according to God's established code—a code that exists outside of any other person's opinion and any other pressing circumstance of life? Or would Adam govern himself according to the urgency of the moment?

See, you and I face a problem when we let our decisions, our actions, and the way we think be determined by any outside force other than the unassailable decrees stemming from the heart of God. We walk through our days with no confidence, no self-assuredness, no self-reliance, and we instead end up relying on the people around us to tell us how we should live.

You know the feeling, right? You walk into a setting that's out of your comfort zone. Maybe it's your first week at that new job. Maybe you're just beginning to attend this new church. Or maybe you're simply showing up at a friend's afternoon barbecue. Wherever you are, you exercise the skill you've become an expert at: self-management. Before you feel comfortable being yourself and speaking up and saying your opinion, you sit back. You reserve yourself and take the temperature of the room, evaluating how John in the corner noticed you when you walked in. Listening to the tone of your new boss as he checks in with your co-worker. Assessing the general opinion of the group regarding the upcoming election before you offer your own opinion.

You take a pulse on what the socially acceptable norms are before you take what feels like the dangerous risk of simply being yourself. Because, you'll be caught dead before you put your foot in your mouth by saying something that people take issue with. You want to fit in. You want to be approved.

While this may seem socially aware and wise—like it's good common sense—it's actually fear. And it's rooted in your lack of identity. Without your Identity firmly in place, you don't know who you are or what principles should even be your driving force. So now you find yourself being governed not by strong, powerful principles, but instead by what people think.

It is impossible to "skip ahead" by neglecting your identity and to go straight to being a Man of Principle. A man who does not know who he is, who his Father is, and who he is in relation to his Father will not find any solid reference point to which he can anchor his principled living. This is exactly why, as you'll see, the symptoms of lack of identity so closely match the symptoms of lack of Principle, especially in the arena of marriage.

ADAM! THANKS A LOT!

As we've seen already, God found it vitally important to give Adam his set of principles before Eve arrived on the scene so that Adam could, if he so chose, establish himself within his God-given code of conduct, independent of her. It was his privilege as a man to live according to the path that God had offered to him, and it was completely his responsibility to stay the course and not be easily swayed by his wife.

Not that our wives are always veering off course and pulling us with them. Not at all. Very often our wives want nothing more than to spur you and me on towards a holier, closer walk with Jesus. But if our whole marital paradigm is one in which we wait to take orders from our wives, whether those orders are good or not, then it doesn't matter how spot-on our wives are. The whole thing is a setup for trouble.

So, *if* your wife does happen to veer off course, like Eve did, it should have no power over you. Adam should have remained sinless. In fact, he should have been such a Man of Principle that he should have spoken up and brought the heart of God into the delicate situation with Eve and the serpent. Not that it would have been his job to control her, but it was his job—which he failed—to speak truth into the situation. Instead, we see silence. The verses even tell us that Adam was with her, yet there are no words.

What was he doing? Kicking back with popcorn and watching? Was he trembling inside because he knew this was trouble, but he was too afraid to make Eve mad? Was he doubting his own convictions and his own connection with God? Is it possible that he was looking to Eve to be his source of meaning and thus his guiding influence? Rather than the word of the Lord and his own set of principles that had come from his intimacy with God.

It looks to me like Adam was playing the nice guy, and because of that he made the worst decision in the history of manhood. Now, you and I have inherited this wicked propensity that we must submit to Jesus and allow him to uproot it from our DNA.

HUSBANDING WITHOUT PRINCIPLE

There are far too many hurting and broken marriages in our church culture today. There are far too many husbands banging their heads into a wall because they can't figure out what happened to the intimacy and passion they used to have with their wives. If you want my honest opinion, much of the advice from well-meaning Christian sources is missing the mark entirely. It's aimed at "fixing" the marriage and altering behaviors, or instilling non-existent ones, with the goal of creating more love between spouses. Good goal. Wrong method.

As husbands, we quite often do not have a solid sense of who God has made us to be: Identity. Therefore, like our father, Adam, we do not operate as Men of Principle according to the code, or principles, that should stem from our connection with our Father. In the void, we almost invariably rely on our wives' shifting moods, affection, and approval to do our thinking, planning, and decision-making for us. We do not say what we think, in love. We don't say what we think at all. We don't present our good opinions and our solid plans for how the next season of life is going to go. We instead cower in fear of speaking up because it might make her angry, hurt, or, you fill in the blank.

When you don't live by your own pre-determined Principle and principles, which you have settled in your spirit in cooperation with Jesus, you will then let your wife's mood at any given moment tell you how you're going to be. If she's happy with you, then fantastic: you too are happy. But if she has an issue with something you've done, then you get, for lack of a more tasteful word, butt-hurt. You get bitter. Maybe you turn inside yourself and shut down. Or you go the other direction and explode in anger. Either way, you're harming your precious relationship with your precious wife because you have, somewhere along the way, decided that you are going to allow the course of your ship to be directed by your woman rather than your Creator.

Does that sound familiar? Instead of getting up each morning and conducting yourself according to the principles that you have decided to value and hold close, do you tiptoe through your day hoping that everything you're doing, thinking, and saying is "right" according to your wife? Have you abandoned part of the core of who God made you to be so that you can keep from rocking the boat and, heaven forbid, causing conflict? Do you typically bottle up your desires and things you are feeling because you don't think she will like them? So instead you've decided to partner with hell in harboring bitterness and resentment in your marriage, and in addition, you accuse your wife of being the one at fault.

I promise you, conflict that arises from your commitment to being a Man of Identity who lives according to Principle is far more consistent with heaven's heart and representative of heaven's atmosphere than this undercurrent of blame and bitterness that's slowly pulling you two apart. Tell me, how is "fixing" your marriage by doing the dishes, bringing home flowers, and having 15-minute connection times going to heal the real problem going on here: your own insecurity, people-pleasing, and fear living openly and unleashed as a man in the Kingdom, under the authority of your Captain?

Put another way, your real problem is that your guiding principle has become, "Keep her happy and approving," rather than, "Love her the way a man is designed by God to love a woman." Do you see the difference? Do you see how one is constantly evaluating her emotional response to your actions in order to figure out whether you're okay or not? The other doesn't answer to her at all. It answers to God alone. And it persists eternally, day in and day out, regardless of her mood and how she feels toward you in that moment.

Which approach do you think will secure her? Which approach do you think will bring you steady peace of mind? Which approach do you think will ultimately make you more attractive? (Let's face it, no matter where we are in our growth into true manhood, we all enjoy our wife's attraction.)

***

Chapter Notes

1) www.dictionary.com. "Definition of Principle | Dictionary.Com." Accessed October 16, 2019. https://www.dictionary.com/browse/principle.

2) "Definition of PRINCIPLE." Accessed October 28, 2019. https://www.merriam-webster.com/dictionary/principle.

3) A-Z Quotes. "John Wayne Quote." Accessed November 4, 2019. https://www.azquotes.com/quote/602672.

5

A MAN OF YOUR WORD, GOVERNED BY PRINCIPLE

BECOMING A MAN of Principle involves not only a separation from your past, leaving behind your old way of living which was merely gaining approval, alleviating pain, and maximizing comfort, but it also involves proactively embracing a new and far better way. To illustrate this new way, I present to you the United States.

I know it is risky to involve discussions of politics and political history in a book like this because so many of us have such heated opinions about these topics. The overactive hyper-emotion that divides and judges others about these things is a sign of lack of Identity, by the way. Though that's not the point here, it's a free warning given in love and with a smile.

Imagine that your old way of living is like democracy. In a strict democracy the fate of a nation is determined by the current opinion of the majority. Unfortunately, that current opinion can be radically errant, harmful, guided by inflamed emotions, sparked by imminent danger or crisis, or maybe just tainted by the voters' recent bouts with the stomach flu. There is no guardrail in place to keep the nation and its people on track. There is no safeguard to protect those in the minority who disagree, who might somehow be hurt in this whole process of steering a country.

Thankfully, the United States' founders were moved to abandon this route in favor of a better way: a republic. One of the facets of a republic is that policy is not always directly decided by the population at large. Instead the populace votes for representatives who are then tasked with the responsibility of making laws and governing. But the more potent, for our discussion, facet of a republic, at least that of the United States, is that it is ultimately governed not by fickle opinion but by a law, a written decree, that is higher than any person in governmental power or not. Ideally, as it is supposed to be, the ultimate authority in our land rests not in anyone's hands, but in the written declaration of who we as a nation have decided to be. The declaration of what **principles** we have decided to value and therefore live by. Essentially, the United States is a nation of Principle—meaning we believe in the power and necessity of living according to a higher creed or conviction—that is governed by principles—laws, guidelines, policies.

Similarly, you have by now made the decision that you are ready to be a Man of Principle who is governed no longer by the changeable circumstances of your life, by the elusive approval of men or of your woman, or by your own shifting feelings. Instead you know that you must be anchored in something higher than any of those: a code to live by that exists and stands true in any kind of storm.

THE INCOMPLETE SECULAR PICTURE

We, as men of the Kingdom, must be careful here. The incredibly powerful and well-intentioned secular masculinity movement, which has been crucial in my own life and to which I owe much of my own transformation, presents only a part of the picture. The secular masculinity movement conveys this idea that we men are to pull ourselves up by the bootstraps. We are to be our own captains, truly self-made men. To an extent, these messages are true. And to an extent, these messages do rescue apathetic, weak, and overly nice men from the mire of impotent living. This movement at least inspires us to finally stand up and make something of ourselves. It lights a fire in us to stop sitting around feeling sorry and defeated. It challenges us to be men—real men—the kind of men that most of us aren't sure even exist anymore.

But as men of the Kingdom, you and I are not the captains of our own respective ships; we are not lone dictators. Our entire fate does not solely rest on our own ability to finally get our act together and make life happen. No, we live in the Kingdom. We are, according to our Identity, sons of God and inheritors of his grace, strength, and provision. While this is extremely good news that frees us from the struggle, the toil, the burnout, the constant striving against gravity that would otherwise pull us to our graves, it comes at a cost.

> "And He said to all, If any person wills to come after Me, let him deny himself [[a]disown himself, [b]forget, lose sight of himself and his own interests, [c]refuse and give up himself] and take up his cross daily and follow Me [[d]cleave steadfastly to Me, conform wholly to My example in living and, if need be, in dying also]." (Luke 9:24 AMPC)

Here is more strong language in the same verse according to the Passion Translation:

> "Jesus said to all of his followers, "If you truly desire to be my disciple, you must disown your life completely, embrace my 'cross' as your own, *and surrender to my ways.*" (Luke 9:24 TPT)

Look at the intensity of Kingdom life. Feel—truly take in and digest—the seriousness of Jesus's words here. Men, you and I are most certainly not in sole command. Rather we are to disown and lose sight of our interests. We are to refuse and give up ourselves. And we are told to surrender to Jesus and his ways, conforming **wholly**—entirely—to him even to the point of dying. Sounds to me like we as Men of Principle are accountable to one who is far higher than we are. We are required as men enlisted in his service to submit to the authority of our King and Captain.

THE INCOMPLETE AND DEATH-INDUCING CHRISTIAN PICTURE

Unfortunately—and I write "unfortunately" emphatically, since we as a collective church culture have largely missed the mark in this and have consequently cost many men their health, their marriages, and their legacies—the church, also, presents a devastatingly incomplete picture of what it means to be a Man of Principle. Too often we tell men that they must live according to God's ways, displaying good Christlike character and turning the other cheek at any possible opportunity, while we simultaneously douse the fire of manly drive, aggression, fight, and passion. We create religious corpses who couldn't rock the boat if they tried—let alone conquer the enemy, bend a bronze bow, or jump over a wall (see Psalm 18)— because they are too busy trying to just be good. They are living up to the rules of religion while their hearts are dying. But if God wants anything from us, he wants us alive and on fire. Otherwise why did he take on death so that we could live?

When you succumb to this overly rule-oriented way of life, you become a bland and boring husband. Excuse me for hurting your feelings, but it must be said. Our church culture of keeping us in line at all times has made us into bland, boring, and unattractive husbands who have lost our "other-ness." As we've tried to follow the rules of "love your wife like Jesus would," "serve your wife more," "remember she's right ninety-nine percent of the time," "make sure she's on board before you jump in," "remember that a primary way God speaks to us is through our wives," and many more such rules, we have lost a part of ourselves. Sure, we have sought to treat her more highly than ourselves, which is very good and the way a Kingdom man should treat his wife, but we have in the process treated ourselves as lower than her, which is not in the Bible and not life-giving.

And what about these other characteristics of "Christian living?" We focus so much on cleaning up our language, and yet we are afraid to yell and shout in excitement about Jesus. We put a lid on behavior that is too risky, dangerous, or unwise, and yet we neglect the fact that we can't find the "on valve" for the rivers of living water that should be flowing out of us and spilling onto everyone we meet. We want to be kind and not offend, but we fail to stand and defend our wife's honor when she is made uncomfortable by someone at church. We are trained to love everyone, but we lose our vigilance over our children's safety around people we don't know. We are told to be wise and safe and prudent with our money, and we walk by broken and hurting souls on the sidewalk.

The church too often teaches slavery to Jesus, which is good and right, without the accompanying freedom that would fuel our hearts to burn with passion. As a result, something is terribly wrong. Our hearts are dead, and it's not the world's fault. In fact, my own masculine heart didn't fully come alive until I looked for help with my marriage outside of the church. I've found that there are only a very few men among Jesus's followers who have been, shall we say, initiated into masculinity. So the fault, my friend, is ours alone, yours and mine, the men of the Kingdom. We are settling for far less than Jesus wants.

THE COMPLETE PICTURE: SLAVERY AND RULERSHIP, DEATH AND LIFE

We must realize that if we are to find the lifestyle we are looking for when we are growing into Men of Principle, then we need to determine our principles both as men under the authority of our King, and as men who have been given authority by the king. And we can only do this as we continue to grow in our Identity as sons, heirs, kings, and priests of God. The errant concept that we are merely "sinners saved by grace" would lead one to believe that he shouldn't be trusted to make decisions, i.e. to powerfully decide what principles he will live by. This kind of man should only ever mindlessly take orders, thereby escaping the threat of making a wrong, sinful, and idiotic decision of some kind.

But when we realize that instead of this, we are washed clean and made completely righteous to the point that we share in Jesus's glory (John 17 and Romans 8) and that we actually **reign with him in this life** (Romans 5), then it becomes much more apparent that we actually can be trusted to take initiative. We can make good powerful decisions about how we are going to live. We can have a say in our principles. And when we get to have a say, we are no longer drones. Instead, our hearts come alive.

For all the scriptures that tell us to deny ourselves, that we are slaves of Jesus, and that we must die, there are others that say the converse.

> Delight yourself in the LORD, and he will give you the desires of your heart. (Psalm 37:4)

> "No longer do I call you servants, for the servant does not know what his master is doing; but I have called you friends, for all that I have heard from my Father I have made known to you." (John 15:15)
>
> "I came that they may have life and have it abundantly." (John 10:10)

And look at the trust that Jesus himself puts in us:

> "If you abide in me, and my words abide in you, ask whatever you wish, and it will be done for you." (John 15:7)

In becoming Men of Principle and deciding what principles will be ours to cling to, we must both submit to the authority of Jesus and also engage our free will to choose. When we understand that we are free to either cling to him or not, then we get to truly come alive and invest ourselves in these principles. Then we find motivation to actually stay true to what we say we believe. We find the grit to stay the course and behave like the man we want to be even when everything around us is pulling at us and tempting us to give in. We stand in the face of trial, in the face of ridicule, in the face of pain and we shout, "I'm not doing this because I have to! I'm doing this because this is plain and simple who I am. I have decided this with Jesus."

NOW WE CAN BE HUSBANDS OF OUR WORD

In this place of healthy principle-forming, where we adopt our code of living that both submits to Jesus and also embodies our own personal dreams, desires, and convictions, we find the ability to stand solid. Remember last chapter, as we were looking at the need our wives have to be secured? To relate with a man who will not waver and alter his behavior or his treatment of her depending on her mood and approval? That man is who you are becoming. You are finding your footing and providing her safety in your submission to Jesus. But you are also finding your voice, your strength, your heart—your balls!—and giving her fiery passion in your coming alive to your own principles and Identity.

This is good. You are looking like your Father. You are ready to become a man of your word rather than a man of your feelings. Psalm chapter thirty, verse five says:

***

> Every word of God proves true; he is a shield to those who take refuge in him.

Look at the power in this verse. Every single thing God ever says comes to pass. It is true. It does not fail or falter. It is not a lie. It is reliable, dependable, and not open to change. When he promises a thing, he keeps the promise. When he says he will do a task, the task gets done.

This is our job as men, to live in such a way that our actions line up with our principles. So that what we **say** we value is proven in how we actually conduct ourselves. This needs to not change according to whether someone in our life hurts us or not. This needs to not change according to whether our wife appreciates us or not. We must remove ourselves from the power that our wives have held over us. And it's not that they have even wanted this. We have put them in this position of perverted power when all they want is to be cared for and protected by a man who stands above them. They do not want the opposite to be true, to be towering above us like the statue of an idol to which we submissively bow.

It is not your wife's job to mother you. It is not her job to tell you, whether directly or indirectly, how to live. That's your job. And if you have given up the job, it's time to take it back. Live according to Principle. Let your words govern your actions. Live in alignment, in integrity.

Watch the second part of that verse, now. It says that God "is a shield" to us when we run to him for refuge. Do you want to know one of the most common reasons for the lack of respect from a wife to her husband? The reason behind her apparent detachment and distance? A major source of her grappling for control in your relationship?

It is lack of conviction. When you lack behavior-guiding conviction, she doesn't know whether she can take refuge in you or not. She doesn't know whether you are reliable and unchanging. Are you someone who will be safe and immovable no matter what happens? No matter what **she** does from day to day? Are you a man who will live with your eyes fixed on who you've been called to be in Jesus no matter what circumstances arise that would threaten to pull you down?

A Man of Your Word, Governed by Principle

When your word proves true and you live according to that word, you become a safe place. You become a shelter where your wife, and a whole host of others who need your protection, can run to. And they can know that you will always be the same. They can depend on you when nothing else feels dependable. And they know that they will not shake you with whatever it is they are currently going through.

If you want your wife to come to you in tenderness and vulnerability, honor and intimacy, where she values your presence and what you bring to the table, then this is a fantastic place for you to begin working. We will jump into this in detail later in the book, but for now, know that you must figure out what principles you are finally going to start living by, regardless of whether your wife sees it and rewards you or not. Ask yourself, given your understanding of your Identity and worth, how is your incredible value as a man and husband going to influence the real and practical way in which you go about your day? You decide. Decide powerfully.

This is not a list of things that you come up with only to submit it to your wife for inspection. Becoming a man of Principle is between you and Jesus. You are looking for your approval and for his approval. That's all.

Let's pause for a moment to consider the idea of your wife's mood and approval. I want to be careful, because it is easy to misstep here and to go from one dysfunctional extreme to the other. One extreme is, in my experience, the more common. It is where you and I abdicate our other-ness, our separate personhood, as we constantly try to manage our behavior so that we constantly gain the approval of our wives and get rewarded accordingly. I think of my dog, Cooper, who obsessively follows me everywhere, constantly staring longingly into my eyes, hoping beyond hope that I will condescend to pat his head, or give him a chicken shred, or throw his ball.

In the same way, you and I can fall into the trap of looking to our wives' affirmation as our sole source of sustenance and happiness. Consequently we alter our opinions, decisions, and behaviors as we pander for her acceptance and try to earn a "pat on the head." Instead of living by Principle, we live under her illegitimate authority, an authority that only belongs to God. In the process, we slowly decay into a bland shell of a husband, thus abdicating our separate personhood, and we fail to show up each day in our full powerful presence, ready to offer what is inside of us to our environment, to bless it by simply being ourselves.

If this is the one extreme—to always let our behavior be dictated by our wife's mood and approval—then the other extreme is to never let her concerns, feelings, and needs influence us at all. This extreme would look more like the macho meathead version of "manhood," which is simply another form of immature boyhood. Here, we fail to treat her with compassion, honor, and love. Here, instead of wounding her by lifting her to a god-like status and selfishly hoping to manipulate her into meeting our needs, we shove her under our feet and trample her spirit under our arrogance and selfishness.

So don't hear what I'm not saying. I'm not saying that your wife's input doesn't matter. She knows better than anyone how she needs to be loved by her man. And part of being a good husband is honoring her and hearing her heart. Part of being a good husband also is being humble and able to hear when you are mistaken. Be ready for the fact that in doing the work to become your own man, a Man of Principle, you might mess up. You might veer off course and accidentally hurt your wife's feelings. So you take the feedback, you hear her heart, you honor her feelings, and you course-correct. Don't hurt her. Don't expose her and neglect your privilege and duty to care for her. Don't aloofly dismiss her insights or feelings or needs. That's too far. That's just as immature as letting her define you.

Instead, we walk the path between the extremes, neither pandering for her approval, nor steamrolling over her heart, and we carry ourselves in confident strength that finds its life source in Jesus and that enables us to truly and deeply love. So you, completely dependent on the guidance of the Holy Spirit —who absolutely will guide you when you seek after him with your whole being—move out of the bitterness-inducing land of living wishy-washy. You **stay** out of the land of jerkish "donkeys" who don't even aim to protect and honor their wives as Jesus would. And you realize that your life up until now has been broken because your highest principle has been to be nice. You've lived to gain approval, whether from your wife or your friends or your peers in work and ministry. You've lived like a ship lost at sea, and you haven't stayed your course.

Therefore, no one has been able to truly take refuge in you. But, thank Jesus who brings complete transformation and healing, because that is all changing. You aren't settling for how things have been anymore. You are new.

THE NEW YOU

I want you to pretend with me that you are in ancient Babylon. You are one of God's people from Judah who has been captured and sent into exile. Even in that land of hardship and pain, where you are tempted to question whether God is with you anymore and whether he is even real, you pursue him. You push in harder to get to know him, for him to reveal himself to you. You and your friends fast, and you stand apart from the crowd because you live by Principle. You pray often and you continue to build yourself up in God's intimate presence. You build your own history with him.

Then you hear about the new law: Anyone who does not bow to the new shiny golden statue when the king's music plays will be executed. But the pressure does not sway you. Threats against your life do not pull your gaze from God and from who you have decided to be, a Man of Principle. So you break the rules. You do not bow to the statue. You worship God alone, and you are called out for it—along with your two friends.

You are arrested and taken to the king, who challenges your "stupidity" and assures you that if you don't bow to his statue this one last chance, he'll crank up the heat in the furnace seven times hotter and then throw you all in. You have no chance of escape. The old you, the immature you, would have crumbled in the name of "reality" or "wisdom" or "living to fight another day" or "choosing your battles." But this you—the you that has been growing roots down deep as a Man of Principle into the soil of God's presence and truth—this you does no such thing. Instead you reply to the king:

> "O Nebuchadnezzar, we have no need to answer you in this matter. If this be so, our God whom we serve is able to deliver us from the burning fiery furnace, and he will deliver us out of your hand, O king. But if not, be it known to you, O king, that we will not serve your gods or worship the golden image that you have set up." (Daniel 3:16-18)

Enough said. You will not budge. You. Will. Not. Bow. Period.

6

MASTER YOUR ALLEGIANCE

I FULLY UNDERSTAND that it's a huge infraction to promote a movie when that movie is actually based on a book. So to all of the literary purists in the world, I apologize. I am about to break that rule. But before I do, I will say with total conviction that every man should be required, upon entering into manhood, to read the great Chronicles of Narnia series by C.S. Lewis. My goodness. What a deep and rich story full of inspiring lessons that many of us do not otherwise receive. And when you have children, please read these stories to them. They need it, and you need it.

Okay. As long as we're good with that, let's proceed. To refresh your memory on the story, there are four siblings: Peter, Susan, Edmund, and Lucy. They stumble upon the mythical land of Narnia by walking through an old wardrobe in an old house owned by an old man. Once there, they meet Aslan, who represents Jesus, and a host of other mythical creatures like fawns, centaurs, talking beavers and bears, witches, wolves, etc.

While wandering in the woods alone, the brother, Edmund, at one point meets the White Witch, who represents satan. Through her bewitching temptations, including the delicious dessert known as Turkish delight, she entices him to betray his brother and sisters and also Aslan himself and to tell her both their location and their plan. Not a good move, Edmund. Not living as a Man of Principle. But that's not the point.

Eventually, Edmund is able to leave the White Witch's castle, and he reunites with his family at Aslan's camp, where a whole army of good creatures, who are loyal to Aslan, are awaiting the forthcoming battle against darkness. Aslan learns, however, of Edmund's betrayal and has a long, private conversation with him, which we never get to hear about. But it is understood that Aslan both rebuked Edmund for what he had done, but he also loved him and restored him, giving him an undeserved place of belonging and honor.

However, because Edmund committed this terrible sin, there is a legal requirement for blood to be spilled in payment. The Witch wants, consequently, to kill Edmund. So she timidly enters the camp, trying to hide her fear of Aslan under an austere exterior and an envoy of evil soldiers, and engages not in battle but in diplomacy with Aslan. She has come to discuss how to satisfy the requirements of the "deep magic," the laws that require someone's blood to be spilled.

She enters into Aslan's tent, alone, just the two of them. And they talk presumably for hours, presumably agreeing to Aslan's proposal that he offer his own blood, his own life, in place of Edmund's. He, like Jesus, would willingly give himself in order to save his precious boy.

The witch finally emerges from the tent looking smugly victorious. She had, after all, just sealed the fate of her enemy and secured for herself a sure victory. She makes her way back to her envoy where her minions are waiting by her pathetic little throne that they carried her in on, and suddenly a thought strikes her.

"Aslan!" She calls out. "How will I know that you will keep your word?" In other words, how will I know that you will follow through on what you have said. How do I know that you aren't lying?

In this powerful, heart-shaking moment, Aslan does not answer her. He is so furious at the question, at the implication that his character would ever be so weak as to allow him to break his promise, that he says no words. Instead, he roars the loudest, fiercest, most terrifying roar you can imagine.

I have had the privilege once in my life to witness a moment like this. It was our wedding anniversary, and we had taken our daughter to the Santa Barbara Zoo to celebrate. It was late in the day, nearly closing time, and most everyone else had already left. We had yet to see the lion enclosure, so we hustled as fast as we could to try to see them before we had to go. Unfortunately, by the time arrived the lions had been tucked away for the evening in their shelters, which happened to be directly beneath the viewing patio. So, we were actually, unknowingly, standing right on top of them. Not long after we arrived only to find the enclosure "empty," we heard right from beneath our feet the most terrifying roar I have ever heard. It was full-force, and I will never forget it. I will never forget the butterflies that swarmed my stomach and the momentary weakness that swept through my legs.

When Jesus says that he is the Lion of the tribe of Judah, it is not a joke. He is not one to be taken lightly.

So Aslan roars.

How dare the witch question his integrity? How dare she question his word?

What a beautiful representation of the character of Jesus. Scripture is full of snippets that prove to us how highly Jesus values his word, the commitments that he has spoken.

> Then the Lord said to me, "You have seen well, for I am watching over my word to perform it." (Jeremiah 1:12)
> "So shall my word be that goes forth from my mouth; it shall not return to me empty, but it shall accomplish that which I purpose, and shall succeed in the thing for which I send it." (Isaiah 55:11)
> For you have exalted above all things your name and your word. (Psalm 138:2)

The New King James Version puts it this way:

> For You have magnified Your word above all Your name. (Psalm 138:2 NKJV)

***

God does not "fly by the seat of his pants" through history, leaving his behavior to be determined by how he feels from one moment to the next. This is what the Witch was assuming. Most likely because this is how she would live her life: according to feeling, to what would seem to be the most convenient or comfortable course of action at any given moment. In fact, God finds it so important to live by Principle that he founded his entire relationship with the people of Israel on a set of written decrees—written in stone. And then, when the time came for the fulfillment of that old covenant, he replaced it with a new covenant written even more authoritatively with the ink of Jesus's own blood.

Declaration, statement of intention, principles are clearly central to God's plan. They are close to his heart. They matter.

In fact, he values his word even above his own name, because it is that word that defines the boundaries of who he is. So your word should similarly set the definition of who you will be. Otherwise, when it comes time to conduct yourself in integrity and honor in your business—when it comes to tax time—if you're leaving your behavior up to the needs of the moment and your low bank account, will you stay the course? Or will you lie and cheat and self-protect?

To be a man, a real man of the Kingdom, your actions must align with your words, just like your Father's. He states clearly that he watches over—the sense is that he jealously guards—his word to make sure that what he declares comes to pass. And he guarantees to us that whatever he has said, it will not be empty. It will indeed come to pass. And we wrapped up the last chapter with the verse from Psalm 30 that assures us every single thing that God says proves itself out to be true. He does not lie. His actions are not incongruent with his thoughts and beliefs. He is a God of integrity, of Principle.

And you are his son. Your Identity is that you are like your Father. Therefore, this must be true of you also. If you say you will do something—if you say you will be honest with your wife, do it. If you say you will take care of your ducks and keep the back patio clean from duck poop, do it. Don't make her keep asking you. If you say you will keep the trash cans from filling up, follow through. Be a man of your word in the small things and the big things. Both are equally important in the Kingdom.

MASTERING OUR ALLEGIANCE

Being a Man of Principle not only involves keeping our word, as our Father does, but it also involves mastering our allegiance, which I'm sure is a term that you aren't familiar with. So what do we mean?

There are a couple places in Scripture that tell us how weighty our words are. Proverbs chapter eighteen says that "death and life are in the power of the tongue, and those who love it will eat its fruit." Now wait. Pause for one moment. Is God really meaning that these two epic opposing forces of death itself and life itself are able to be influenced—even determined—by the words that you and I speak? Isn't that kind of power reserved for Jesus? It doesn't look that way. I'm sorry, but God isn't going to let us escape this responsibility he has given us.

It sounds extreme, overdone, and melodramatic—if we're being honest with ourselves—but this is not some crazy mystical new age magic. This is Kingdom. This is in alignment with God's intentions. The words that we say shape our history. They shape the course of our lives and the development of circumstances that we see from day to day.

Let's go one step further into "absurdity" and apply the same truth to our unspoken words: our thoughts.

Wait, what? Our thoughts shape reality?

Yes.

For as he thinks in his heart, so is he. (Proverbs 23:7 NKJV)

Your thoughts are the precursor to the actual, tangible, physical readout of your being. Your thoughts shape your character. Your character shapes your actions. Therefore, your thoughts write your story.

If all this is true, then you and I had better be very careful, considerably more careful than we have ever been. We say that we believe Jesus and that we follow him, but do we? If the constant narrative in your mind is contrary to his word of joy, power, and hope, then are you truly loyal to him? Or is your allegiance actually given to hell? I'm not saying that your salvation or your standing in the Kingdom and in God's heart is in question. But yes, your allegiance is definitely in question. My allegiance is in question.

Since our words and our thoughts, which so easily and quickly turn to principles that are contrary to God's heart, carry this incredible amount of power, to choose life or death, then we had better make sure they align with where we want our allegiance to lie: with Jesus. As Men of Principle, we must master our allegiance by mastering our thoughts and words. Not only do they influence our own inner life, but they shape the course of events in the spirit realm in a way that many of us do not yet realize. And the spirit realm shapes the physical.

When we give our allegiance to darkness by thinking dark thoughts, we will see darkness play out in our experience. Do you know what that means? It means you need to cut the head off of thoughts like these:

-I am a bad husband.
  -I am a bad father.
  -I am incapable of truly providing for my family.
  -I always screw up.
  -I will never be free of pornography.
  -I will never have my wife's desire, respect, or sexual attraction.
  -My body will never get healed.
  -My wife is so cold.
  -My wife is so distant.
  -My wife just doesn't want sex anymore.
  -Our marriage is hopeless.
  -I don't have anything to offer at work.
  -I'm not cut out for more than this.
  -I'm not fit for ministry. Leave that to the gifted ones.
  -My insight and what I have to say aren't worth much.

* * *

These seemingly innocuous and seemingly true thoughts that you've allowed to play over and over from day to day completely unchecked are actually killing you. They are inviting the demons of hell to come and eat you for lunch, because by thinking them, you are declaring that, in these arenas, hell has your allegiance. Even if heaven has your heart! So wake up, soldier! Wake up! It's time to stop giving in and giving up by letting yourself think and say whatever you feel in the moment. I don't care what history has taught you. I don't care how many times you've failed in the past. I don't care how many times you've been hurt in the past. I don't care how many times you've tried to get closer to your wife only to get rejected.

Do you think it's okay to give up and let your experience tell you what God's will must be? Excuse my language, but hell, no!

Literally: "Hell, no! No more!"

Simply because your body hasn't been healed yet, that doesn't give you the right to think that it's not God's will for you to be healed. Tell that to the father who came to Jesus in Matthew seventeen after the disciples couldn't heal his boy. He would tell you, "My son wasn't healed when the followers of Jesus tried to pray for him, but as soon as Jesus himself entered the scene, my boy was instantly healed." The lack of healing did not define God's will. God's word defines his will.

Just because your finances have been in the hole for your entire adult life, does that give you the right to start thinking that God's will for you is lack and poverty? Or do you think that maybe his word stands truer than that, that God supplies all your needs according to his abundant riches? Your lack of money does not define God's will. His word does.

Just because you've fought with your wife over and over for the past several years, seemingly never getting anywhere, and your heart feels tattered at this point, do you think that it's okay to start thinking thoughts of blame, accusation, and bitterness toward her? Does that give you the right to make her the villain of your heart? Or should you search the Scriptures for yourself to find that God actually says in Proverbs that she is your crown? Your marital pain does not define God's will. His word does.

Thinking these thoughts that so readily present themselves as we face trials and pain is actually you going toe to toe with Jesus in the ring. He said that anyone who isn't for him is against him. There is no middle ground here. So let's, together as men of the Kingdom, get our heads on straight and take the reigns of our lives back from satan and his horde. We had better know what we believe and what we stand for in every area of our lives. Otherwise we're going to be like waves tossed around by the wind. And that weakness has no place in the life of a man. That is not the life that will pan out the way you want it to. I guarantee it.

This is why, if I'm struggling in a certain area of my life and I feel like it's not adding up to what it should, I do the work to find out and decide what principles I will live by in the midst of it. One prominent area like this for me is my health and physical sickness. In my twelve year battle, I have done everything known to humanity that can be done to combat disease. I have gone to about twenty doctors, done treatments of all kinds, adopted every nutrition plan available, and sought healing at the hands of Jesus himself. But at the core of all of that, I need to know what is driving me. Circumstance that isn't panning out? Or Jesus? And by Jesus, I mean, his word—his principles.

For you, it's time for you to go to the wrestling mat with him, open up his word, and ask the Holy Spirit to talk to you. Build your own history with him. Ask him to show you what his will is for you in your pain, outside of the crappy circumstances. Search out the Scriptures. Wrestle with him in prayer: "My life is broken in this area, but there's too much at stake to just stay bitter. I've got to figure out what I'm going to believe. What I've been believing up until now is broken, and it has been in allegiance with darkness. And God, I want you to have my allegiance again. I want to replace my dark narrative with your Truth."

This does not mean that everything that goes wrong in your life is directly your fault. Nor does it mean that if all of your thoughts and words are on point, then it will be the magic formula that automatically makes everything better. I'm not proclaiming that fixing your life is simply a matter of emphatically declaring good words. It's not a matter of using Bible verses as coins in a vending machine to purchase the right results. It is not a math formula where you put in x and you get out y. But at the same time, if you do not have mastery and dominion over your words, thoughts, and beliefs—over your allegiance and what kind of man you are going to be—then you are setting yourself up for some very hard crashes in some very dry deserts.

You and I cannot build a solid structure if the foundational words beneath are broken.

TAKE ACTION

If you are hurting somewhere, if you feel wounded in battle, then be a Man of Principle and go and open up the Bible and find what the Holy Spirit wants to say to you about that pain and about that area of your life. When I found what He says about sickness, it shaped my thoughts and words, and I consequently decided who I was going to be—even though my circumstance was painful. If you are hurting in your marriage, figure out what God has for you and your wife. Because being stuck in hopelessness will get you nowhere. You need something outside of you, God's code of conduct, his principles, to pull you out. You need truth that exists independent of you and independent of your wife.

If you don't have enough money to get by, and you **never** have enough money to get by, then search out what God says to you about your money. Find his will for your work, success, prosperity, and calling. See what his thoughts are about creating wealth.

Again, stop letting life determine for you what you believe. Stop letting people determine what you believe. You decide. With Jesus. You must do the work and go to Jesus saying, "What do you have to say about this painful part of my life? It feels like I'm off, like I'm living broken." It's quite possible that what you're believing is right on. Maybe your allegiance has been with the Lord through it all. Good. Stay the course, and do not let yourself get swayed. But if you find that you've been missing something, that you've been off and your allegiance has been with your enemy, then stop.

Stop those runaway thoughts of:

-Things are never going to change.
   -I hope today is different than yesterday.
   -This is just the way it is.

***

If life and death are in the power of your tongue, then it's time for you to stop speaking death over your life. Stop speaking death over yourself, over your kids, over your finances, over your future. Stop speaking death over your wife. She's God's daughter, and you are wounding her.

Instead, find the eternal truth that has come from your Creator and declare his principles. Speak life:

-My past does not determine my future. All things are made new.

-God forgives all my iniquities and is faithful to cleanse me from all unrighteousness.

-For freedom, he has set me free (Galatians 5:1)

-My family is a gift and a blessing.

-I have more than enough, and God will give me all things, whatever I ask in his name.

-My wife is a gift.

-I am a gift to her.

-I am worth her time and attention and affection.

-I will change the world.

Agree with these things that come straight from Scripture. Choose these principles even in the face of the doubt that rears up and yells at you, "That all sounds really great, but it sure feels like a load of crap!" You persist and you stay your course. This is what it means to be a Man of Principle. This is powerful living. This is the manly strength you've been looking for. This is how you become the man you didn't think you were cut out to be. Trust me, brother, you are a man among men. You belong in the circle of initiated men, men who know who they are—the power, authority, worth, and image they carry—and who know where their allegiance lies—in the principles of God.

Declare what is true even in the face of everything telling you that it's a lie. The Bible, your field guide, tells you that all enemies are being made subject under the feet of Jesus. So there might be some rebellious elements of creation out there that you are facing. There are elements that don't line up yet with his rulership. Do not take it lying down. Somehow we have thought that this is the way to do life: to let our circumstances defeat us, dictate what we believe, and determine our future. But not anymore. We are going to be Men of Principle, and we are going to stand and declare God's truth in the face of darkness.

You may have a history that has worked against you. You may have pain and hurt. You may have delusional thoughts of self-worthlessness and people who have wronged you. You may have downright crappy circumstances choking the life out of you. Even so, now is the time to stand and, with your words and thoughts, steer your ship. You don't have time to waste anymore. There is too much at stake. You have a whole mission that God is eagerly waiting for you to fulfill. You are too valuable to be stuck in your self-pity, licking your wounds.

PRINCIPLE IN ACTION

This is why I take so seriously how I live out the principles that God has revealed to me in his Word. I'm not just working to be a good Christian man. I'm not looking to check off the boxes of requirements, completing my tasks so that I can be deemed "good" and win the endearingly titled "Jesus award" all four years of high school. True story. That happened. But the reason I take this seriously is that I will not live half-in and half-out of anything. If I have declared what I am going to believe, and therefore what will determine my behavior, then I'm going to be true to my word the whole way through, one hundred percent.

One obvious arena where you and I come face to face with this is in our money. I say that I'm going to believe God about money, and his Word promises that if I seek his Kingdom first—meaning, if I make God and his character and his desires in the earth my all-consuming passion—then he will take care of everything that I need (Matthew 6). He will clothe me, feed me, shelter me, and he will do so abundantly. His Word also says that if I give him the first portion of all of my income, then he will pour out an amazing blessing on me so that I won't even be able to handle it (Malachi 3).

This becomes extremely difficult to adhere to during times when the money is not there, and it doesn't seem to even be anywhere in the near future. When we don't know how we're going to make it to the next month, these principles that God has established do not feel true. And if I were a man who lives by my feelings, I would not feel like giving any of my money away. I need it! So my actions would reflect those feelings, and I'd hold on tightly.

But I've lived that way. I've lived small, where my primary aim is survival and self-protection, and it only leads to death, lack, and despair. It does not lead to a life of miracles where I know the joy and excitement, the adventure, of seeing God show himself strong on my behalf, proving his power. In fact, just the other night, my wife and I were discussing some dreams that we have for the next stage of our life together, and she asked me if I thought we were ready. Did I think that we would actually be able to handle the things we were hoping for?

I answered her, "Absolutely. We can absolutely handle it."

She replied lovingly to me with a smile on her face, "Well, you are kind of insane." She, of course, didn't mean it derisively at all. She was just saying that I often seem to be out of touch with reality when it comes to life plans and dreams.

But I told her, "You know, though? I've lived 'not insane.' I've lived by what feels wise according to less-than-favorable circumstances where life looks a certain way, and so we'd better tighten up and hunker down. That kind of living leads me into small, selfish self-protection, which is toxic and harmful to you (my wife). It's not good for me and not good for you. So yes, we can handle this. Let's go for it. God is with us."

Jeremiah chapter thirty-three assures us:

> Thus says the Lord: If you can break my covenant with the day and my covenant with the night, so that day and night will not come at their appointed time, then also my covenant with David my servant may be broken. (vs. 20-21)

In other words, "You can't change what I have said I will do. You can't break these words of mine, so put me to the test. Go ahead. I will follow through. As sure as the sun rises and as sure as the sun sets, I will follow through. And if anyone questions this, they are in for a surprise."

When I live according to Principle, I get to take a stand against the world declaring, "You know what? Come life or death, screw it. This is who I'm going to be. So bring whatever you've got, but I will not change. And if God is real, then he will prove himself on my behalf." And it's true, God will see this kind of principled living and he will endorse you. He will back you with the full force of heaven so that nothing from hell's arsenal will take you down. Join me in this. God will be faithful. He will meet you in your risk, as you live as a Man of Principle.

PART THREE: A MAN ON MISSION

"A man needs a much bigger orbit than a woman. He needs a mission, a life purpose, and he needs to know his name. Only then is he fit for a woman, for only then does he have something to invite her into."

-John Eldredge[1]

7

RECLAIMING YOUR FIRE

I sat in our local coffee shop, uncomfortably navigating the interaction between my exceptionally bony butt and the less-than-ideal rock hard chair, waiting for my next appointment to come in. I was working at the time as a private tutor for high school students who needed help navigating the challenges of school, and my next student was admittedly one of my favorites. He was a young man who went deeper than just math homework. He had been through some "stuff," made some bad choices, and wanted someone to connect with him beyond his mistakes.

He walked through the doors on time and sat down heavily at our table against the wall. The distracted and pained look on his face told me something was wrong.

"How's it going?" I asked.

"Oh man, not good. I just came from basketball practice, and I'm pretty sure I have a concussion."

"No way! What happened?"

"I was going up for a rebound while my friend was on his way back down and his elbow crashed right into the top of my head. Hard. I've had a concussion before and this feels exactly the same. I'm nauseous. My vision is blurry. I can't focus. It's really bad."

I chose not to ask him why the heck he came to meet me instead of going to the doctor, and I engaged a newly developed narrative in my mind that Jesus had been leading me into. Over the last few months I had begun to realize that there was more to my experience of the kingdom of God than I had known before.

Pause.

Remember the story I shared with you in chapter two, about my health journey? How I had been bedridden and from that place began to seek God's heart about the topic of physical healing? This coffee shop encounter took place shortly after that fresh awakening that God led me through, when I was (and still am) in a major battle for my health. To refresh your memory, this health battle involves an extremely aggressive condition that has pained and damaged my joints, caused pain throughout the rest of my body, made me lose weight and height, and tried to steal all good things from me and my family. And as I write these words, it has been raging for twelve years.

In that awakening, when my Father initiated me into a new aspect of my Identity as a man who is healed and whole, in whom sickness has no right, God also planted Mission in my spirit. Not only was I understanding that healing is mine as a son of the Father, but I also began to realize that I could and probably **should** pray for others to be healed as well. After all, I couldn't deny these verses staring me in the face:

> "Heal the sick, raise the dead, cleanse lepers, cast out demons. You received without paying; give without pay." (Matthew 10:8)
> "And these signs will accompany those who believe: in my name they will cast out demons; they will speak in new tongues; they will pick up serpents with their hands; and if they drink any deadly poison, it will not hurt them; they will lay their hands on the sick, and they will recover." (Mark 16:17-18)

"Truly, truly, I say to you, whoever believes in me will also do the works that I do; and greater works than these will he do, because I am going to the Father." (John 14:12)

"For truly, I say to you, if you have faith like a grain of mustard seed, you will say to this mountain, 'Move from here to there,' and it will move, and nothing will be impossible for you." (Matthew 17:20)

See, in the midst of my pain and seeming defeat—in the midst of sickness looking like it was about to have its way with me—God did something momentous. He reached into my spirit, or burst up out of my spirit (whichever is more accurate), and he planted a new Mission inside of me. Instead of leaving me inside of myself and inside of my situation, he sparked a fire to go. Go! He urged me, "Go out, Matt, and in your war against the sickness in your own body, this enemy from hell, push back the darkness that has crept into others' bodies. Bring to them the healing of my kingdom."

Both suddenly and also gradually, I was initiated into this Mission of healing. My mind no longer sat in toxic stagnancy, stewing over my pain. I began to have a vision for the future, a vision for what **could** be. And I had a battle to fight rather than a defeat to accept.

So, fast forward to this day in the coffee shop with my student who had just come in with a concussion. As he told me about his condition, my mind was going berserk with thoughts about healing. My heart pounded faster. My breathing quickened. I was nervous. And I thought to myself, "This is it. This is the moment. I have a choice to either back up what I say I believe with actions, or I can play it safe and do nothing, carrying on with tutoring him through his math as normal."

What kind of man did I want to be? One who is afraid to truly engage authentically with the world around me, always tiptoeing around apologetically and never acting on what I believe about Jesus? One who is more concerned about my own comfort level than God's kingdom? Or would I be a Man on Mission who risks boldly and takes whatever consequence may come? Would I be a man who lives more to fulfill my kingdom calling than to preserve my false sense of dignity?

I made the choice and jumped in.

"Listen, you might think I'm crazy, but would you mind if I pray for you right here in the coffee shop?" I knew it could be awkward and embarrassing for him too, but oh well. This is where we were, and Jesus probably doesn't care so much about embarrassing situations.

He answered, "Sure."

So I did. I prayed for him discreetly and quickly, "Jesus, thank you for loving this young man. Thank you that you love and bought his body with your own blood. Thank you that you want to show him your love right now. So in Jesus' name, I command his head to be healed."

When I finished, I asked him if he felt anything, and he said, "No."

So, with his permission, I prayed again, not changing anything about my prayer, just attacking this thing with persistence. When I finished the second time I asked him again if he felt anything, and to my surprise as much as his he said, "Yes!"

"What? What do you feel?"

"This second time when you prayed for me, I felt a cold rush come over my head, and as the cold came and left, the pain went with it. It's gone. I feel fine. I can see fine. Thank you!"

And with that, I was hooked on Mission. That, my first ever experience of a healing miracle, was the ignition point for a lifetime of going after healing both in my own body and in others'. I have since seen dozens healed and hope to see dozens more. No longer was my health battle simply a dark valley for me to just put up with, where I hope desperately and powerlessly that God notices me—because that's how I had felt. But now, this health battle was the fire in my spirit that pushed me to **go**. Up from my sickbed, I stepped into Mission.

DESIGNED FOR MISSION

> God blessed them. And God said to them, "Be fruitful and multiply and fill the earth and subdue it, and have dominion over the fish of the sea and over the birds of the heavens and over every living thing that moves on the earth." (Genesis 1:28)

* * *

At the outset of man's existence, before we men had the opportunity to be lulled into complacency by the comfort of our home, God says to us, "Go." Go! Do not stay put. Life was not meant to be one long vacation where our hardest work and most valiant efforts are spent building walls to keep trouble out. We were not designed to live out our days in one of those huts built on top of the shallow lagoon, hundreds of feet from the tropical island shore. As tempting as it is to find a paradise and to settle, allowing room, or hut, service to bring us our tropical fruit breakfasts and mimosas, a life like this is contrary to our God-given DNA. And as such it is death.

A man is designed to be on Mission. He is designed to wake up each morning with eyes fixed outward—outside of his bed, outside of his home, outside of his mind. You, sir, are designed to live for far more than your dignity, comfort, and well-being. Your goals should amount to something more than just an end to the struggle.

God says to go, to be fruitful and to produce, to leave an impact on the world. He challenges us to multiply. Yes, we all love the one obvious interpretation of this mandate, to go get with your wife and have children. But there is more here than simple procreation. God is challenging us, challenging you, to increase. We are to expand the territory that we are currently living in. God's intent was never for Adam to stay in the garden. Not at all. He was to treat that garden as his command center, his headquarters, the place to which he could return after going out and conquering.

Multiply.

In other words, "Take my image that I have deposited into you—your identity—and replicate it over and over in the earth. Bring my mark into every corner of creation. Wherever your foot lands, bring my kingdom to that place."

For me, this was getting up and out of my self-pity and despair over the sickness that was attacking me. It was re-orienting my focus onto Jesus my King and his kingdom. It was going and multiplying in others the reality of his healing power. It was multiplying his presence in an otherwise dark world so that he could bring transformation.

It is time for you to understand that simply working to "get by," to "make it," to survive—it's not good enough. It's not good enough for God and it's not good enough for you. The world and the time in which you live, the time you were intentionally hand-picked for, needs you. If you do not go out and live in your full calling, then the rest of us will suffer because of it. God is calling you to bring his peace and order and kingdom into a world that is waiting for you.

HELD BACK BY BAD THINKING

But how many of us persistently sit back and refuse to do anything with our lives? We are held to the comfort of our cushioned chairs by the lies that whisper to us, saying we don't have much to offer. All that we're cut out for is making a living, and we all know that's hard enough on its own. Forget about anything resembling a Mission, a call to live beyond mere survival.

We believe that the world doesn't need us, and so we are the fortunate ones to be allowed to exist. We are borrowing our time here, and we are glad that the world has condescended to make a little bit of room for us to mind our own business. What often accompanies this inert existence is one giant apology to the world. We apologize—if not with our words, then with our tone and actions—for getting in the way, for rocking the boat too much, for having the audacity to assert something.

Our mantra becomes: "Could I just trouble you for this little piece of land, or this house, or this apartment? I'll only need it for about seventy years. I'll do my best to not get in your way."

Does this sound familiar to you? Then consider this your wake up call. This is dangerous territory that you need to vacate immediately, because it will set you on a very damaging course for each day of your life. Instead of waking up and, at the outset, being geared towards offering value, you will gravitate toward survival and self preservation. You will be consumed with self-focused obsessions. How am I going to **get** today? I hope that today goes better for me than yesterday. I hope that today my wife shows me she's attracted to me. I hope that our finances change. I hope that something happens to me to change my difficult situation.

These thoughts, though they feel important and even justified, are opposite to how a man in God's kingdom should think. As a man of value and worth —as a Man on Mission—you should be asking a completely different set of questions. Your obsession should be: How am I going to **give** and bring value to my world today? How am I going to bless the people I am with today? How am I going to give love and pour out for others?

The instant you connected with Jesus and told him you were all in, he initiated you into something so much greater and more deserving of your time than your self-serving manipulative attempts at feeling better in life. Your attempts at soothing that inner ache that stems from your insecurity. Your constant focus on how to simply "be okay" and how to get your wife to fulfill you again. You, man, were told to crucify yourself and die to your own way. You were told to lay it all down for the sake of answering one who is far greater and more worthy than anyone or anything in your life. You were hand-chosen to enlist in the Captain's army and to engage in advancing his kingdom and pushing back darkness.

MARRIAGE: MISSION VS. MANIPULATION

When we are caught in stagnant survival mode with no Mission we evaluate each person, yes, especially our wife, and each circumstance according to what they could potentially do to us. Can they offer me anything? How can they help me? What's in this relationship for me? What will I get out of it? Or we cower in fear while we worry about how the person or circumstance could potentially harm us. And when we let this overtake our thinking in our marriage, we find ourselves baffled and wondering why we've somehow magically lost the admiration of and connection to our wives.

But what is there to admire? What is there to be connected to when the only energy you are operating in is self-advancement and self-preservation? How is she supposed to want to connect with you and open herself up to you in warmth and vulnerability when your default mode of operation is manipulation? Yes, manipulation. I can see the cringing, and I can hear the objection: *Manipulation! I'm not manipulative! I'm not sitting around and conniving about how to maniacally steer the world in the direction of my choosing.*

Excuse me, but yes you are.

Manipulation can be blatantly obvious, like when the melodrama villain dressed in black with his curly mustache schemes about how he's going to take over the world from his underground lair. But more often, it is a sinister undercurrent, a colorless, odorless poison that secretly fills your atmosphere and slowly starts killing the people you love.

Manipulation is in full force when your thoughts drift toward yourself and you no longer live according to Principle or on Mission and you selfishly conduct yourself in a manner that is designed to achieve your desired results, whether from people or circumstances.

Do you know how damaging this is to your marriage and your wife's heart? On her end, she feels your manipulation in full force. She feels that everything you do to "love" her is actually a tactic for you to get what you want back from her. She never gets to simply enjoy being loved and adored and cherished, because she feels a constant expectation attached to your behavior. She feels a constant worry about what you're going to secretly expect from her now that you're being such a good husband.

So she's not feeling loved. She's not being filled up. Instead she feels resentful toward you.

On your end, you start feeling like you're going insane because you're "trying" to love her. You're "trying" to show her how much she means to you, how amazing she is, how sexy she is. She always used to respond warmly to your displays of affection. What happened? Now, you're doing all of these loving acts and romance-inducing gestures, but you're not getting anything in return. You feel unloved, so you start to feel hopeless and, like your wife, bitter.

The problem thus far is that you haven't realized that you've been operating on top of a broken foundation, a foundation laced with manipulation, where all of your actions carry the unstated goal of self-gratification. Your vision has been focused far too low and far too close to your home base. You are making your life's work revolve around your marriage, and while that is certainly your most important human relationship, it must not be the central focus of your mental and physical energy. No woman wants to be her man's mission, her man's adventure, her man's all-consuming purpose. This is simply another form of idolatry where she is worshipped and supplicated and elevated above her man. But what she wants is to be swept into the man's adventure and mission. She wants a man who is driven by something bigger than either of them. She wants there to be fire in his eyes for her, yes, but also for the passion and purpose for which he was created: knowing Jesus, kicking out darkness, and advancing the Kingdom of heaven.

You become stuck in toxic cycles in your marriage, your work, your thought life, and your spiritual life because you don't realize—or you haven't until now—that you were made for Mission. You were not designed to sit back and have things handed to you all the time. If you want to get something out of this life, then you'll need to go out and conquer.

> In all these things we are more than conquerors through him who loved us. (Romans 8:37)
> I can do all things through him who strengthens me. (Philippians 4:13)

What you'll receive when you begin to live this way is the satisfaction and fulfillment that comes from the act of conquering. Your behavior as a Man on Mission will be reward in itself. Your living this way will be satisfaction enough. Any positive response from your wife or others around you is merely icing on the proverbial cake. Because what you are truly feasting on is the personal growth and confident security that comes from becoming who Jesus made you to be: a real man who is more than a conqueror and who has strength to do anything.

He didn't equip us with supernatural power and authority and his very presence so that we could sit back and do nothing in our lives beyond appeasing ourselves. Nor did he equip us for overcoming so that we could merely live in the ethereal world of "someday." Someday I'll chase down that calling. Someday I'll reconnect with my wife and kids. Someday I'll mow the lawn. Someday I'll get to that dream that's been latent and crushed. Someday I'll finally engage with God again. But none of these things will happen today because I don't feel like doing them. They are uncomfortable, and without living on Mission, my highest priority is my comfort.

I'm sorry to tell you, but not sorry at all, your Mission starts right now. You do not have time to lay around in "somedays" anymore. You are equipped to carry out your Mission, to be a Man on Mission, starting today, this very moment.

So stand tall and lift up your eyes. Look further out. Fix your gaze toward the horizon. That is both where you are heading—because on Mission you are also pioneering and taking new ground—and it is also where your answers, your fulfillment, and your meaning will come from. What does the Psalm say?

> I lift up my eyes to the hills. From where does my help come? My help comes from the LORD, who made heaven and earth. (Psalm 121:1-2)

On Mission, you connect with your Creator. This is a sacred connection that no other human has access to. On Mission, you climb the mountain to meet with Jesus your King, your Captain, and you come back down glowing with his presence and alive with passion for his service. On Mission, you delight in inviting your wife into the adventure, but you do not make her the pinnacle of that mountain.

START SOMEWHERE

We see Adam's Mission show itself again in Genesis chapter two, verse fifteen:

> The LORD God took the man and put him in the garden of Eden to work it and keep it.

What's interesting is that God said previously in chapter one to go into the entire earth and subdue it. That is very much outside the borders of a garden. That Mission, to fill the whole earth and take dominion over it, was clearly too big for one man to do all at once. But Adam had to start somewhere, so God placed him in the garden and told him, "Start here. Work it and keep it." While this may not have been the entire earth, "working" and "keeping" still sound a lot like taking dominion.

God is telling Adam, "Hey, this garden needs you. It doesn't operate in its full potential on its own. So get to work. Care for it. Bring order to it. Cause it to produce at its full capacity. Don't just sit on your butt and pick fruit every time you're hungry. Work and be productive. This is part of your Mission, and the earth will suffer if you don't live up to it."

And we catch another piece of Adam's mission in verse nineteen:

> Now out of the ground the Lord God had formed every beast of the field and every bird of the heavens and brought them to the man to see what he would call them. And whatever the man called every living creature, that was its name. (Genesis 2:19)

This is all before Eve enters the picture, a fact which, again, is extremely important for us men who are so susceptible to being dazzled by our wives' hotness. (Let's be honest, beauty doesn't fully do it justice.) It's almost as if God sat Adam down, knowing that he was about to introduce him to the most stunning element of all of creation, and presented his manly Mission to him before he had a chance to get distracted by Eve. I can hear the Fatherly admonition now:

"Listen, son. You're about to see something you've never seen before, and she is going to be so mesmerizing that you'll be tempted to make her the center of your existence. Don't do it. That would not be good or healthy. But before she gets here, I want you and I to get on the same page. You have a Mission, a calling, a high purpose of reigning on this earth that only you can fulfill. Invite the woman who is coming into your leading and pioneering on this adventure. Do not elevate her above your stature. She needs you to stand over her and protect, cover, and honor her."

Another life-changing point that John Eldredge makes in his book *Wild at Heart* is that a woman wants to be swept up into an adventure. But she will grow tired, weary, burdened and resentful when she becomes that adventure. Is your Mission merely validation from your wife? Tell me, what is there in that for her to attach herself to? You want her to love you, to respect you, to adore you and be affectionate towards you, but what in the way you are living is fostering those behaviors from her? This goes back to the problem with lack of Identity. If you're just a chameleon looking to do whatever it takes to blend into the current mood, then you are not presenting the confident, strong Man on Mission that God actually made you to be.

If you have found yourself living your life **not** on Mission, and you've lost that fire, the glint in your eye for the horizon, the unknown, the something greater, then let's get that back. Let's follow the example of our King. The book of Isaiah prophesies about Jesus that he "set [his] face like a flint:"

> But the Lord God helps me; therefore I have not been disgraced; therefore I have set my face like a flint, and I know that I shall not be put to shame. (Isaiah 50:7)

And take in for a moment the full force of these various translations of Luke chapter nine, verse 51. They communicate beautifully the attitude, the grit and fortitude, with which Jesus went after his Mission of redemption:

> Now when the time was almost come for Jesus to be received up [to heaven], He steadfastly and determinedly set His face to go to Jerusalem. (AMPC)
> When it came close to the time for his Ascension, he gathered up his courage and steeled himself for the journey to Jerusalem. (MSG)
> Now it came to pass, when the time had come for Him to be received up, that He steadfastly set His face to go to Jerusalem. (NKJV)
> Jesus passionately determined to leave for Jerusalem and let nothing distract him from fulfilling his mission there, for the time for him to be lifted up was drawing near. (TPT)

Jesus knew his Mission, and he steadfastly and courageously, with dogged determination, set his face toward it until he accomplished it. Does this describe you? Are you following his example? Have you received the vision for your life Mission by going into the place of prayer, the place of wrestling it out with God, the place of being alone with him until he implants it into you? We must understand why we are on this earth so that we can come out of that secret place of prayer completely on fire. We enter into the consuming fire of God himself and we come out of his presence still on fire, burning with passion just as Jesus did.

Nothing can change us now. Not lack. Not sickness. Not pain. Not attack. Not success. Not failure. Not the approval of men. Not the approval of our wives. Not angels. Not demons. Nothing.

Leave behind the mission of approval. Leave behind the mission of validation. Leave behind the mission of comfort. You must awaken your drive.

It will not happen on its own. You join with Jesus in the process. I challenge you right now to get alone with God and tell him, "I'm sorry, God. I'm sorry that I haven't lived on Mission. I have settled for less, and I've sat back waiting for you to do everything for me when you are all the while asking me to stand up and go."

Second Timothy chapter one, verse six commands us to "fan into flame the gift of God which is in you through the laying on of my hands." So fan it into flame, brother. Fan into flame the gift of your Mission. God will empower you and meet you in the process, and he will even slap you in the face to get you moving. He will encounter you in surprising ways that will change your life, even through this book. But this does require movement from you.

In Jeremiah chapter twenty-nine, verse thirteen, God invites us, "You will seek me and find me, when you seek me with all your heart." In other words, "Come get me."

When you engage with him and step into the river of his presence, you will see him. You will hear his calling to you. You will get the fire for Mission burning inside of you. But if you don't step in, you will be left on your own, either doing life as you have been, making lesser things and people your mission, or conjuring up your own mission which will leave you pursuing it in your own strength and eventually burning out.

But when you do step in to his presence in this way, you must be all in. In the same way that Jesus was our example in setting his face like flint toward his Mission, he now is our example of "going all in." He gave everything already. He poured all of himself out so that he could have all of us and we could have all him. So you must do this and stop holding on to life like you have been, regardless of consequences.

When we come to Jesus, we are coming into a Kingdom that is not about building our own self-serving empire in this life. It is instead about him and who we are becoming in him. In this Kingdom we live with abandon, fully unleashed no matter what may come because we are now in the grip of the King. We are now in our Father's hands. So we live by the power of the Spirit and we get to see amazing, epic moves of God, miracles from him—literally, the kinds of events that make the unbelievable but captivating plots of the best movies.

If we take hits along the way, so be it. We are soldiers in an army, warriors in a battalion who are following a Captain. We are not living high up in a castle tower, but down on the ground taking more territory against the enemy.

As this type of thinking begins to grip us and flow through our veins so that it reshapes our DNA, we become incredibly winsome to others around us. Yes, we'll turn some people off by our uncomfortable and outlandish living, but they won't be able to deny that there is something alive and passionate, vibrant and full of vigor, inside of us that not many other men have. We will be adorned with the very same qualities that have previously caused us to be envious of other "more manly" men. Remember how the old you used to watch epic movies with men like William Wallace or Robert the Bruce or Maximus, and you'd wish, "If only I were like him." Well, now you can be.

This is the life that Jesus offers. God gave you a "spirit not of fear, but of power and love and self control" (2 Timothy 1:7). So step into this new, but ancient Identity of yours as a Man on Mission. Do not sit back on the sidelines afraid of failing and of what someone is going to think when you begin to transform. Do not let fear of the unknown, of taking on scars, of royally screwing it all up, stop you. If you are living in fear then you are living outside of your DNA, and it's time to repent to Jesus, ask him to help you break free, and believe something new.

Pray to him, "Will you help me? I give you permission to do something in me. I haven't seen you do much, and what I have seen was a long time ago. But Jesus, the way I've been doing it isn't working. It isn't who I am. Now it's starting to have a readout in my life's brokenness. So will you make me, as I join you in the process, into a man full of power and love and a sound mind? I want to have dominion over myself."

If Adam started close to home in the garden as a part of his bigger mission of taking dominion of the earth, then your close-to-home-garden is inside yourself. It is this DNA level transformation into a Man of Identity, Purpose, and Mission. You've got to work that land and keep it because you've been letting it grow wild. Like my own back yard when I don't get out there and show it who's in charge, you've let your inner man succumb to the weeds popping up everywhere. It's time to clean it up and get it in order because God has bigger dreams for you.

***

Chapter Notes

1) A-Z Quotes. "John Eldredge Quote." Accessed November 4, 2019. https://www.azquotes.com/quote/1316270.

8

HOW TO BE LEGENDARY

THE WORD *MISSION* has two important meanings, and it is essential that a man's life displays both. The second should always spring from the first. Mission means:

> 1) an important goal or purpose that is accompanied by strong conviction[1]
> 2) any important task or duty that is assigned, allotted, or self-imposed[1]

The first definition is clearly a more grand or universal and overarching concept of Mission. It is intangible and qualitative, describing the type of life that we want to be living day in and day out. It is this instinctual gut-level drive that pushes us onward through every circumstance. My own Mission at this stage of my life is this:

> To know Jesus and be known by him better today than yesterday, and better tomorrow than today. From that place of continual revelation

and intimacy, to pour his presence and power into every corner of my life and my world. Starting with myself, then my wife, then my children, then every person I meet. To make him and his Kingdom my all-consuming passion so that everything I do is drenched in him, and I am constantly pushing back darkness while taking ground for the Kingdom.

See how this Mission is completely unrelated to a specific job or task? I can be on Mission like this while I am sitting here writing. I can be on Mission while I am working in my backyard. I can be on Mission while preaching the gospel to high schoolers. I can be on Mission while praying for a sick man on the sidewalk to be completely healed. I can be on Mission while I'm reading my girls a bedtime story. I can be on Mission while sitting and listening to my wife's heart at the end of the day.

This thing follows me, and I keep it always before me. It consumes me, and I love it.

The second definition of Mission, "any important task or duty that is assigned, allotted, or self-imposed," conveys the smaller, more practical meaning. And we need this too. After all, what good is a big grandiose mission without a way to actually flesh it out. Rhetoric and philosophy that sound powerful and manly do not serve anyone if they are not met with action. And that action can take shape in an infinite number of ways, depending on how God has built us. What's more, that action, the smaller Mission, can look different at different seasons of life.

Right now, one of my missions is to write a total of four books, including this one, by the end of the year.

Another is to convey more and more to men in the church that there is a better way, a Kingdom way, to be a man.

Another is to reach teenagers with the message of the gospel that shows them Jesus is worth everything they have to give, and they too are worth everything Jesus had to give.

Another is to take dominion over my yard.

Another is to get my body healthy, finally.

Another is to pray for others who are sick and see more healing miracles.

Another is to buy my wife a home.

Another is to return the blessing to my mom and free her up so she can stop working.

All of these are temporal, dependent on the current situation, and are subject to change as I achieve them. But all of them fit well within my overarching Mission as described above. Ah! I love this! Men are meant to connect with God's heart, as the prophets, seers, and priests of old, and to embrace his thoughts as their own. But then we are also meant to put action to that heart. Right? Isn't that what Jesus asks?

> "Go therefore and make disciples of all nations, baptizing them in the name of the Father and of the Son and of the Holy Spirit, teaching them to observe all that I have commanded you. And behold, I am with you always, to the end of the age." (Matthew 28:19-20)
> "Truly, truly, I say to you, whoever believes in me will also do the works that I do; and greater works than these will he do, because I am going to the Father." (John 14:12)
> But be doers of the word, and not hearers only, deceiving yourselves. For if anyone is a hearer of the word and not a doer, he is like a man who looks intently at his natural face in a mirror. For he looks at himself and goes away and at once forgets what he was like. But the one who looks into the perfect law, the law of liberty, and perseveres, being no hearer who forgets but a doer who acts, he will be blessed in his doing. (John 14:12)
> So also faith by itself, if it does not have works, is dead. (James 2:17)

And remember Adam. He was given his large-scale mission of taking dominion over the earth and multiplying God's image everywhere he set his foot. But then he was given a "so start here" mission of tending the garden. Visionary, and practical. So, you, as a Man on Mission, must be driven by this one creed that resonates with every cell and strand of DNA in your body. And that creed then drives you into all of these various avenues so that you can live out that creed, whether they be jobs or chores or hobbies or ministries or relationships.

This is one way where you get to be the portal of heaven coming to earth. Do you realize that? Jesus was that very portal, bringing the presence of God to the earth in the form of a man, but now he says that we are like him. He is sending us into the world just as the Father sent him. We get to walk just as he walked, and we, his servants, are like our master. So now we are this connecting point between God's will in heaven and God's will actually being done on the earth. We get to watch him work miracles completely supernaturally, and we get to become his miracles by living in Identity, from Principle, and on Mission.

This is a privilege and an honor that must not be passed over anymore.

WELCOME TO LEGENDARY

Don't you want the Bible to stop being a collection of other people's legendary stories and to start being your reality? I used to wish I was alive in Bible times because I was told that "God doesn't do stuff like that anymore." But now I read its words, and I pray, "God, make this my life more today than it was yesterday! Do not let me be limited by old religious thinking. Do not let me be limited by what's impossible. With you all things are possible."

This philosophy of life, where we plug ourselves into God's power source and higher calling, if we are doing it right, will always promote us out of the mundane and the comfortable and into the exciting and **un**comfortable. This type of living requires us to part ways with the easy and more acceptable way of just getting by. I'm not saying that you have to leave your job for the mission field. But are you willing to bear the reproach, reprimand, and possible termination that may come when you make your job your mission field? Or maybe for you, you **do** need to leave your job for the mission field. There is no formula to adhere to, only fire for the leading of the Holy Spirit. A Man on Mission lives by this verse from Isaiah, no matter the path it leads him down:

> And your ears shall hear a word behind you, saying, "This is the way, walk in it," when you turn to the right or when you turn to the left. **(30:21)**

We no longer live by lists of pros and cons, by housing markets, by the opinion of friends and family, by what's "wise" and "prudent." We live in a way that looks reckless to the world, following a still small voice that even we sometimes wonder about. We may be tempted to wonder if it's actually God's voice or if we are simply delusional and making it all up. But the fruit will prove: we are not delusional, simply supernatural. If we sat for coffee, I could tell you story after story of God's faithfulness to show up when I took the risk of following his leading. He has paid me money from nowhere when my bank account was empty. He has given me a free car. He bought my wife's engagement ring. He has given me a word of knowledge for one of my students about a knee, and it turned out that his mom's knee had a cyst. We prayed for it, and she was healed.

My wife and I have moved across the country after praying for two months to hear from God a simple "Yes, move," or "No, don't move." When we finally heard him say "Yes," in our living room while listening to a sermon from Times Square Church, we packed up everything and moved completely across the country, watching our money multiply to cover the costs. He gave me another still small whisper and told me about the birth of our first daughter before she was even conceived, just so I would know that I'm hearing from him.

To the outsider, this is crazy and irresponsible. But to the one living on Mission, taking orders from our time spent with Jesus in the Captain's tent, this is normal life. A Man on Mission understands that his only duty is to pursue passionately the things that Jesus is pursuing in the manner that Jesus would pursue them. To live by any other guideline, for any other purpose, is mundane, boring, and where the true danger lies.

NOAH

Noah is one of the first examples we have in Scripture of a Man on Mission who is promoted out of the mundane and into the epic. He is told by God in Genesis chapter six that a flood will soon come to destroy the whole earth. So Noah is supposed to build a giant boat that will preserve his family and every species of the earth's animals. That is crazy. Noah did not just automatically do this. He was given a choice. He did not have to follow this leading. He could have simply carried on with life as normal. In fact, he probably should have. Certainly he had plenty to do already to take care of his family, whether he needed to hunt or farm or battle, I don't know. But it's not as if he had been sitting back waiting for something to do.

It was quite irresponsible of him to use more of his precious survival time to now build a giant boat for a flood that may or may not come. The only thing he had to rely on in this was God's voice. He was truly walking by faith. But you and I know that it surely would have been far more dangerous for him to live by comfort and by what he could see. If he had taken this easy route and denied his Mission, he would have been swallowed up like the rest of the earth.

ABRAHAM

Abraham, several generations after Noah, also sacrificed his comfort for the sake of his Mission. God told him to get up and leave his father's house, way of life, and entire homeland to go to a place that Abraham had never before seen. He had no idea what kind of home God was leading him into, how he would make it work, where the provision would come from, and if he'd have enough money to pay for the local property taxes. But he went anyway, into the unknown, following a voice: crazy.

Even though he doubted and sinned and tried to force God's promises into fruition rather than trust God's timing, he was given a promised son because he followed God. A miracle baby. Crazy.

Moreover, following the voice of God again, Abraham led that same son up a mountain fully prepared to kill him as a sacrifice to God, because God had asked him to. Insane. God stopped him, by the way, and provided a ram for the sacrifice instead. God always wanted for Abraham's son to live. But he also wanted Abraham's heart of supreme devotion. It's as if God is saying, "Abraham, even when you've received the things precious to you that you've been hoping for, will you still be a Man on Mission?"

I'm not advocating that you go out and do the stupidest things you can think of. Nor am I arguing that following God means that you intentionally live reckless and that you try to do things in the most uncomfortable way possible. Not at all. That's foolish. But living on Mission does mean that you have to be willing to follow his kind, challenging, loving, Fatherly, uncomfortable voice no matter the cost.

***

"In the same way, those of you who do not give up everything you have cannot be my disciples." (Luke 14:33)

YOU CAN BE A MIGHTY MAN

Your life can look this way—full of risk, victory, adventure, miracles—all the time. And this life is open to you regardless of where you have come from or where you are at now. That's right. Most of us battle pesky tenacious thoughts that we are not qualified to be quite as much "man" as others. We believe that heroic adventure should be left to the protagonists in the movies. We watch while other men sweep a woman off of her feet, and we wonder why we don't have the same ability. What are we missing?

You must stop letting the pain and disconnect—disfunction, even—in your marriage tell you that you are a failure as a man. You must stop letting your struggle to make ends meet, to keep putting food on the table from month to month, tell you that you do not have what it takes. You must stop living your masculine adventure vicariously through fictional, mythical, historical, or famous men. Stop disqualifying yourself with stupid and immature thoughts of, "Poor me. This is not for me."

No more.

Have you heard of David's mighty men? They were a group of the fiercest, most formidable warriors history has known, and the Bible records many of their near god-like feats. But they did not begin in such a glorious fashion. Not at all. The book of First Samuel, chapter twenty-two tells us:

> David departed from there and escaped to the cave of Adullam. And when his brothers and all his father's house heard it, they went down there to him. And everyone who was in distress, and everyone who was in debt, and everyone who was bitter in soul, gathered to him. And he became commander over them. And there were with him about four hundred men. (vs. 1-2)

This was at a time when David was running for his life from King Saul, who out of jealousy wanted to kill David. David was an outcast, living on the outskirts of society, a man with no home and no support and no visible way to ascend to the throne that God had said would be his someday. He had nothing. And into this nothing, these four hundred men, who had each reached the end of their own respective hopes, gathered.

What a picture! At a time when David could have used professional soldiers with know-how, experience, and raw savage ability, he gets the scum of the day: men in distress, men in debt, and men who were "bitter in soul." These are not the men that you want on your team. These are men with baggage, with grudges, with problems that you don't want to have to deal with. But also, they had nothing left to lose. And a man at the end of himself with no other options is a potent force to be reckoned with, if he so chooses.

If you so choose.

And these men saw something in David, a faint source of hope. They saw an opportunity to stand up and out of themselves and their problems. They saw a Mission that was bigger than what they had known. And like them, you do not have to have any piece of your life put together at this moment, the moment of your transformation. You can be in the deepest pain you've ever known. You can feel like you, far from being an epic hero, have epically blown it, and more times than you remember. You might be messed up and far from Jesus and unable to figure out how to fix it.

No matter the state you find yourself in, you are qualified to join the ranks of this King, Jesus. He will not leave you in your current state. When you join him and become a Man on Mission, he completely transforms you, just as he does in your Identity and Principle. The book of First Chronicles chapter eleven gives us a later glimpse into the lives of these used-to-be outcasts and low-lifes:

> Now these are the chiefs of David's mighty men, who gave him strong support in his kingdom, together with all Israel, to make him king, according to the word of the Lord concerning Israel. (vs. 10)

This is you. You are a chief of the mighty men of Jesus. You are tasked with the honor of giving him "strong support" in his Kingdom. You are to reign with him, propelling his rule throughout all of creation. We do not become Christians just so that we can have one foot in and one foot out, trying to use him to build our own empires. We enter into his ranks so that we fulfill our God-given destiny of making him known. Just as these men abandoned their old lives, their old broken ways of trying to make something of themselves, so also are we to abandon our previous lives, lives that were only sucking the life out of us anyway.

LIVING BEYOND THE 9 TO 5

When we enter into Mission completely abandoned, not loving our lives even to the point of death (Revelation 12:11), we are ushered into an entirely other plane of life. No longer do our dreams only amount to making a living. Our lives are meant for more than being able to put a down payment on a house. Our lives are meant for more than the next promotion at work. Our lives are meant for more than making it to the weekend so we can finally live a little. And they are certainly meant for more than showing up at church on Sunday so we can get our God-fix.

Please understand, none of these things are bad. None of them should be villainized. God loves the good gifts, and he delights in giving them. He does not want a total denial of the physical needs and wants that you and I have, in some show of religious and self-depriving loyalty to an austere God. Not at all. In fact, he wants to lavish more pleasure, more gifts, more happiness and joy on us, his sons, than we have yet known.

But too often we elevate these above Kingdom living. We put on hold the war against darkness and the rescue mission for lost souls until we have our 401(k) lined up.

Our lives are not first for those things, and then for Jesus. Our lives are first and only for Jesus and his Kingdom. From there, he lavishly provides every possible good gift, spiritual and natural. And he can more freely do this now, because we have opened ourselves to becoming men of his nature and character. Men who can carry the weight of both battle and blessing, and not crumble in the process. And from this missional heart stance of counting everything else as loss compared to him, we can then go out and secure a living for our family. We can do battle to build a home for our wife. We conduct ourselves with excellence in the affairs of life because they are all part of this greater purpose to bring the Kingdom of heaven to earth.

Living on Mission doesn't excuse us from our duties as men. Instead, it uplevels us. It brings us to the top of our game because we now pursue them in health, knowing that they are simply part of the bigger Kingdom picture of our lives. We do not run after them in panic and obsession. We do not hustle and grind to make it through. We walk in peace and rest, understanding our victory in all things is already won. We show up. We deliver. Kingdom come.

Did you notice how bad@** the men who strongly supported David were? One of them killed three hundred men by himself. Another took a stand after his companions fled, to defend a plot of barley against the Philistines. He fought so fiercely that his hand literally clung to his sword. Another killed a few hundred Philistines by himself. And still another, Benaiah, was known for killing two "Moabite heroes," for jumping down into a pit to kill an unsuspecting lion, and for stealing an Egyptian giant's spear only to kill him with it.

These are all men who were disqualified and shouldn't have been included in the king's closest circle. They were in distress, in debt, and bitter. And yet they were enough. And you are enough for the Mission in front of you. You're exactly the right man for the job.

You feel like your wife doesn't love you. You're the right man to love her.

You feel like the dream in your spirit of building a ministry or business to impact the world and set people free is too big for you. You're the right man for the job.

You feel like your kids are out of control, and there's nothing you can do. You're the right dad for them.

Your neighborhood is hurting. You're the right man to bring them Jesus.

There's a person limping down the street. You're the right man to go pray for them and to see them healed right there.

For anyone—literally **anyone**—walking down the street, you're the right man to tell them Jesus loves them.

This is not for somebody else. This is for you.

FEAR IS NO EXCUSE

Think with me way back to Gideon. Remember that God gave him a new Identity in the midst of his fear? Chapter six in the book of Judges goes on to describe how God then gave him his first Mission: "Hey Gideon, go pull down the idol that's standing in the town of your family. It's in opposition to me. I hate it. I'm asking you to be the one to overthrow it in my name. And then I want you to set up an altar to me and offer sacrifices to me. Redeem this land."

Remarkably, the Scripture says that Gideon, though he was seeing God face to face, was still too afraid of his family and the other townspeople to fulfill this Mission during the day. So he waited for the secrecy of night, and then timidly, but obediently nonetheless, went through with his task. And God, ever the irrational one, does not even mention this. He doesn't hold it against Gideon. He doesn't rebuke him for his lack of faith. Instead, it's as if he considers Gideon a successful graduate, and he promotes him on to his more spectacular mission of saving the whole nation from the Midianites.

You, Man on Mission, do not have to be perfect at this. You merely need to step into the ring. You don't have to be fearless and confident and strong—that will come. You just need to believe that you can become those things, and you need to start walking towards them by stepping in to this life that Jesus has for you. You do not have to feel your "awesome-ness" in order to be awesome. You do not have to feel your confidence rising in order to gain confidence. You do not have to be perfect for God to think you're amazing. He already thinks it and sees in you every manly quality you thought was long gone.

Are you going to believe him? Will you take him at his word, no questions asked? Will you stop protesting, "But God—?" You've already been doing that, and it hasn't moved you any closer to your heart's desires.

YOUR COMMISSION, THE FAITH OF OUR FATHERS

It's undoubtedly a bit strange of me, but I'm going to leave you with something to think about that should get its own set of chapters. Instead, I'm only going to give it the last portion of this last chapter. Maybe this thought will find its own book in the near future.

Here, one more time, are the two separate "Great Commissions," as we know them.

* * *

"Go therefore and make disciples of all nations, baptizing them in the name of the Father and of the Son and of the Holy Spirit, teaching them to observe all that I have commanded you. And behold, I am with you always, to the end of the age." (Matthew 28:19-20)

"Go into all the world and proclaim the gospel to the whole creation. Whoever believes and is baptized will be saved, but whoever does not believe will be condemned. And these signs will accompany those who believe: in my name they will cast out demons; they will speak in new tongues; they will pick up serpents with their hands; and if they drink any deadly poison, it will not hurt them; they will lay their hands on the sick, and they will recover." (Mark 16:15-18)

Jesus here brings us full circle back to the garden, where he originally told Adam to go and take dominion over the whole earth. Except now our Mission is not only to build his Kingdom, but to **rebuild**. We are being called to reestablish and repair and set back into order the things that have been marred by sin and satan and sickness and death and all forms of darkness. You can see, if you take these commissions at face value, that the full picture of this Mission involves not simply saving souls, but also doing miracles in the earth—miracles to set people free from darkness and sickness.

I'd like to challenge you to lay down any denominational differences and to try this. To risk stepping into the miraculous power of Jesus. After all, if we make it our aim to become Men on Mission, but we purposely neglect this primary—this foundational—Mission, then what are we even doing? For too long our culture has robbed us of the epic adventure that is Christianity by telling us that these things aren't for today, that we are being presumptuous and arrogant to think that **we** could heal anyone, to operate by the leading of the Holy Spirit and confront demons when they show up. Instead we've inoculated ourselves with a watered-down doctrine-centric body of head knowledge. But Jesus did everything he did, and still lives today, so that we could join him in a real, living, vibrant collision of heaven and earth. We should not expect it to be comfortable. But it is good.

The Scripture goes on to tell us that these disciples went out and preached the gospel and that Jesus confirmed their words with signs and wonders. The book of Acts, chapter four, shows them again asking God to renew his presence, as it were, and to perform more signs and wonders through them. We have this same privilege, to call on our Father to show himself strong and powerful on our behalf. We get to join with him as we go and conquer. We get to be legendary.

ONE FINAL STORY

Throughout my health journey, I have received treatments of various kinds. For a season I was driving forty-five minutes every six weeks to Stanford Hospital to receive infusions that would keep my symptoms at bay. On one such day, I had just finished my three-hour infusion and was hustling as fast as I could out of the infusion room so that I could get to the bathroom. Three hours of liquid being involuntarily poured into you will "encourage" you to visit the restroom afterward.

But on my way down the hall to the restroom, I saw a woman in front of me, limping with crutches. Immediately, the battle began. Do I go to the bathroom to find the sweet relief I had been waiting for? Or do I pray to Jesus that he helps me make it a little longer so I can go catch up with this poor woman? I made my choice, and my bladder is stronger now for it.

Foregoing the restroom, I rounded the corner of the hallway, catching up with the woman just in time to join her on the elevator ride down.

"What's going on with the crutches?" I asked.

"A couple months ago I was hit by a car while walking, and I broke my femur."

"Wow! I imagine, based on the crutches, that you're still in pain?"

"Yeah," she sighed. "It still hurts, and I have to keep coming to follow up appointments to make sure it's healing."

This woman looked like she needed healing. She had clearly seen some rough days in her life. She had several tattoos, somewhat messy hair, not the nicest clothes. Her visage, at first glance, was cold and uninviting. But as she and I talked, I could hear sincerity and pain in her voice. I could hear a softness that she probably didn't often express.

I asked her, "Would you mind if I pray for you? It doesn't matter what you believe, and where you've come from. I know that Jesus loves you a lot, and he wants to show you by healing you. Could I pray for you?"

Surprisingly, she awkwardly but willingly said yes. It seemed like she at the very least appreciated the gesture of someone stopping to care about what she was going through.

The elevator hit the ground floor and we made our way off to the side of the lobby, out of the way but in plain sight to everyone walking by. Not wanting to embarrass her, I made my prayer quick and discreet. I slightly bent at the waist and reached my hand toward her knee, but didn't touch her at all. And I prayed quickly, "Jesus, thank you for loving her. Thank you that you bought her body on the cross, and that you want to show her your love and power. In Jesus' name, I command this leg to be completely healed."

I stood back up and asked her, "Do you feel anything? Be honest with me, don't make anything up just to make me feel good."

She looked stunned. "That was weird. I felt someone touching my leg, but I know it wasn't you. I saw; you didn't touch me at all."

Smiling and excited, I told her, "That was Jesus holding your knee. He's healing you. Thank you for letting me pray for you."

I started to make my way out of the lobby, happy and excited both that I took the risk to pray for this woman, operating in courage fitting for a Man of the Kingdom, and also that Jesus actually showed up and did something. But as I was about to walk through the doorway, I heard her exclaim behind me.

"What the heck?! I swear my knee hurt before!"

I turned to see her looking at her leg in amazement. She was just now realizing that, in addition to the spooky feeling of some unseen reality touching her knee, the pain was actually gone! Maybe Jesus really did heal her.

I walked back to her and she met me with teary eyes, unable to hold back her amazement, "Thank you, thank you. You are so blessed."

"No," I corrected her, "I'm not the one who's blessed. You are. Jesus healed **you**. He loves you. You are blessed."

"Thank you," she repeated. "Thank you for giving me a story to tell when I get home."

WHAT STORY WILL YOUR LIFE TELL?

Will you join me and step into the ranks of Men on Mission for their King? Will you allow Jesus to turn your mundane everyday routine into opportunities for battle, for loving passionately, for healing sickness, for setting captives free, for experiencing his presence? Will you stop fixating on your immediate surroundings and lift your eyes to the hills, to the horizon? Will you go to God and in prayer receive from him your Mission so that you can stop making your wife that Mission? Will you invite her into your adventure? Will you model for your children what a Man on Mission, a man living completely beyond himself, looks like? Will you show the world what a man on fire for Jesus looks like in flesh and blood?

This is not just ancient words on the pages of ancient Scripture. Answer the call. Rise to the occasion. Now is your time.

***

Chapter Notes

1) "Mission | Definition of Mission at Dictionary.Com." Accessed October 31, 2019. https://www.dictionary.com/browse/mission?s=t.

CONCLUSION

When learning something new and having corners of our heart reopened after years of disuse, it can be frustrating to try to figure out exactly **how** to go about changing. This is both the strength and weakness of Christian preaching, writing, teaching, etc. One sermon—or one book—can be exactly the word of the Holy Spirit for us in that moment. And we need no clear explanation of how to implement the word. We need no step-by-step guidance to move from point A to point B, from the brokenness we've been in to the victory that's now presented to us. There are many times in my own life when this has been my reality. The inspiration and supernatural power of the word in its perfect season was enough to empower the transformation almost effortlessly, on its own.

Sometimes, even if the lasting effect of a certain message is not quite as acute as that, the fact that our eyes are now open to a new idea, a new way of living—even if we don't yet know **how** to do it exactly—is all we need at the moment. The inspiration is in itself sufficient for what we need, and the "how" comes gradually over time.

But there are those times when we need the "how." We hear a message that is truly life-changing, but we are left wondering, "How do I actually become a man like this? It all feels so out of my reach. If I knew how to get there, how to be a Man of Identity, a Man of Principle, and a Man on Mission, I would have done so already. What do I actually do?"

This is no small task. You are looking to shift from an orphan with no Identity to a son who walks in belonging, confidence, love, and power. You are looking to shift from a wishy-washy man guided by the moods and approval of others, to a man who is steady and strong and driven by Principle. You are looking to shift from living small, and aiming only to alleviate your pain and create more comfort, to living legendary as a Man on Mission for his King.

The only effective way to engage in these massive shifts is to engage with the Lord himself. You might be feeling bitter, frustrated, and hopeless. You might be believing that the Lord will not actually affect your life. If your life has been a mess up until now, and you haven't seen him swoop in to rescue you, it makes sense that you'd feel that way.

Or maybe you're fine with God, but you're still ready for a new season—a new level—of relating with him. You're ready for a new experience of his powerful presence in you.

Wherever you are, the only way to fully embrace your new life, based on your ancient DNA, is to literally engage with him in your day. Take time, physical effort, and emotional energy to enter into conversation with him. Sacrifice something for the sake of connecting with him. You may not receive immediate answers, but that's okay. Welcome to manhood. One of our essential qualities is grit, where we don't give up. Ever. Quitting is not an option.

So you have to decide right now, what path are you going to take? Maybe it will be a different path, one that is other than finding your Identity, Principle, and Mission in Jesus and your Father. That's your choice. I can't stop you, but I know that it will not be the most helpful route, and it will leave you constantly toiling and running dry. Your Creator is the one who gave you your DNA, so you should probably discover all of its power and subtleties in step with him. And whatever the case, you had better not quit.

Jacob wrestled with God all night long when he was under the threat of death. All night. That's a seriously long time to continuously wrestle. When you think that your situation is never going to end and it seems like God isn't answering, that's wrestling all night. You might have to just keep going. You might have to muster that last bit of impossible strength and endure until the dawn hits.

Do you know what happened at the break of dawn? As the sun shattered the shadows, God's words shattered Jacob's old life and give him his new DNA. God gave Jacob a new name, and with it a new inner reality. God will do the same for you, but you've got to jump in and hold nothing back. You have to make finding your place in his heart your all-consuming pursuit.

PRACTICALLY SPEAKING...THE CAMPFIRE AND THE BATTLEGROUND

Life-change in the Kingdom of God happens primarily through two avenues that we must cultivate together. We do not choose one over the other, we embrace both. Like the two edges of a single sword. Keep in mind, while it sounds simple, each of those two sword-edges has infinite possible variations and total potential for adventure. God does not operate in a system or a box. He is creative and not limited by our explanations. However, what I'm about to lay out for you is concrete enough to actually give you some tangible footholds.

Life-change—finally experiencing the power of your manly DNA—happens, first, with the supernatural power of God operating in you apart from any effort and strength that you'd ever be able to muster on your own, and, second, with you going to battle and fighting with all your strength. Since you are a warrior, and when you come to Jesus and begin life in his kingdom, you are enlisted into the ranks of his military, you are invited both to fight on the battlefield and also to return from that battlefield to sit with him at the campfire. Your transformation and experience of God's power happens in both places: around the campfire and also on the battleground.

When you are sitting at the campfire, resting from the day, you're not fighting. You've set your weapons down, and you let down your guard, peacefully resting in the presence of Jesus, your Captain. He is excited to join you as he too rests by the fire. You eat, tell stories back and forth, and possibly even let him clean your wounds and put you back together. Here, you are simply being with him, experiencing the thoughts on his mind and the goodness in his heart as you share your own deep thoughts, and connect meaningfully with him—taking the risk of letting him truly know all of you, pleasant and ugly alike.

My campfire, in real life, involves me getting up early in the morning, before anyone else in the family is awake, except for maybe my dog, Cooper, and going outside with my journal and my Bible. I dedicate separated time to seeking Jesus. I dedicate my physical action of going to a dedicated place to seek Jesus. I call on my entire being to engage with the act of pursuing his presence. I don't just lay there groggy in bed. For me, that's not seeking him with my whole heart (Jeremiah 29:13) or loving him with all my heart, soul, strength, and mind (Luke 10:27).

During this time, I do two things primarily: I listen to God's voice from the Scriptures, and I pray. These may be two cliche and seemingly outdated modes of relating with God in an age of needing something novel and exciting, but I know of no other more reliable ways to actually meet with him face to face. I know of no more reliable ways to build the kind of relationship that replaces religious duty with experiential reality. This is how we become shaped by him and have him miraculously transform places in us that have long been hopeless. Commit to seek him. In prayer. In his word. In the Spirit. And in truth.

Regarding the battleground, this is where we are tasked with taking what we have received from God, and exerting our own will and strength to actually start believing it. On the battleground, we go to war and engage our loyalty and agreement either with Jesus and truth or against him in favor of the lies of hell. This is what we were learning in chapter six.

It's easy to hear the word "war," or "battle," and to immediately dream about changing the world, feeding the hungry, healing the sick, and all of those good, grand-scale, external things. But they are not the war you need to fight in order to be transformed into the Man of your God-given DNA. No, your initial and fundamental battleground is your mind. The war is for your thoughts, words, and beliefs.

This is vital because it's far too easy for us to spend time around the campfire with Jesus, only to step out onto the battlefield where we continue to agree with all of the old toxic thoughts and principles of darkness that kept us living defeated. It's possible for us to spend time with Jesus but to keep living according to the old narrative. Without our direct effort to go to battle, the thoughts from satan will consume our minds, take over our beliefs, and direct the course of our lives—even though we're saved.

Stepping onto the battleground means proactively choosing what thoughts you will allow in your mind and what words you will allow out of your mouth. You begin the discipline of declaration, proclaiming either to yourself, or to your family and friends, or to the spirit world, the truth of God about who you are as a man. You pick up and wipe off that old rusty sword of the Spirit (see Ephesians 6), and you christen it with the blood of the enemy as you finally fight back against the chaos that had been running rampant inside. This is you living on Mission as you take dominion over your core, your DNA.

You may find that you need to consciously rehearse and declare the truths of your Identity, Principle, and Mission constantly. You may find that being vigilant against the thoughts of darkness is actually exhausting because they attack so much. Maybe a more appropriate picture here is one of swinging an ax at a tree. Perhaps this is not a case, at the moment, of you warding off enemy invasions as much as it is you slaying dark strongholds that have over time taken root inside you.

Nonetheless, over time, you will find that your war becomes easier, almost effortless. As you clean up your inner man while also, at the campfire, filling in the barren landscape with the life-giving water of Jesus, you begin to take dominion over more and more ground. You rebuild your defenses that had long been in ruins.

> They will rebuild the ancient ruins and restore the places long devastated; they will renew the ruined cities that have been devastated for generations. (Isaiah 61:4)

Get strong, as a man should be. Get unshakeable, as a man should be. Become a refuge for your wife and others, as a man should be. This is why you are here, to rebuild every part of yourself, your life, your family, and your world that has been battered and shattered by the onslaught of darkness.

Fight back against the disillusionment. Rise up above the noise of your feelings, and believe again that he has not in fact forsaken you. You are not alone. Your Father, the one whose image you carry, is right here with you. And he will, as you seek him, show himself strong on your behalf.

I'm telling you, there's more. It is time for us as men to go and take it. You have to find it for yourself, for the sake of your survival. Find it for the sake of your family. Find it for the sake of the Mission that you have been called to.

So step into the extreme power of your DNA as a man, and, in the words of Nehemiah, "Let us rise up and build."

JOIN MATT HALLOCK AND THE MAN WARRIOR KING COMMUNITY

In the coming months, the Lord is going to grow the ministry of Man Warrior King as the Lord and I together develop new teaching resources, live seminars and conferences, and more depth in our podcast.

I'd love to have you jump on board and join us in what God is doing. The book of Malachi tells us that God's desire is to turn the hearts of the fathers to the children and the hearts of the children to the fathers. This is what we are going to see at Man Warrior King in the months to come.

So, head over to the website and sign up to be in the in-crowd with other like-minded men who are recklessly pursuing Jesus.

WWW.MANWARRIORKING.COM

DID THE DNA OF A MAN CHANGE YOUR LIFE?

If you have found this book and any of the other work by Matt Hallock and Man Warrior King to be powerful in helping you to become every bit the Kingdom man that you are meant to be, would you please head over to Amazon and leave a review?

If you feel like this book has helped you discover new aspects of yourself, a new way of approaching your marriage, a new way of thinking about your role in the Kingdom and in walking in God's power, would you tell others about it?

Reviews are crucial in helping others find these books and in enabling me to continue the ministry and message that God has given me.

Thank you. I'm very grateful to you.

ABOUT THE AUTHOR AND OTHER WORKS

Matt Hallock is on a mission:

> To know Jesus and be known by him better today than yesterday, and better tomorrow than today. From that place of continual revelation and intimacy, to pour his presence and power into every corner of my life and my world. Starting with myself, then my wife, then my children, then every person I meet. To make him and his Kingdom my all-consuming passion so that everything I do is drenched in him, and I am constantly pushing back darkness while taking ground for the Kingdom.

I am currently pursuing this mission through my work as an author, my work with high school students, and my work with Christian men. This is my second published book. The other is:

More Than Standard—Written to empower high school students to walk in the full power of the gospel. In the book, I show teens how Jesus can practically and impactfully free them from depression and feelings of worthlessness as he leads them into living like conquerors. All with an academic bent.

Amazon author page and author website:

WWW.AMAZON.COM/AUTHOR/MATTHALLOCK

* * *

About the Author and Other Works

WWW.MATTHALLOCKAUTHOR.COM

See what I'm doing to bring the Kingdom of God into the lives of high schoolers at my website:

WWW.MORETHANSTANDARD.COM

See what I'm doing in the lives of Christian men at:

WWW.MANWARRIORKING.COM

Made in the USA
San Bernardino, CA
21 December 2019